LAVENDER LAND

Lavender Land

A Mémoire

Jo Anne Wilson

MISSION POINT PRESS

Readers are encouraged to go to
www.MissionPointPress.com to
contact the author or to find
information on how to buy this
book in bulk at a discounted rate.

Published by Mission Point Press
2554 Chandler Rd.
Traverse City, MI 49686
(231) 421-9513
www.MissionPointPress.com

ISBN: 978-1-943995-56-1
Library of Congress Control Number: 2018934961

Printed in the United States of America.

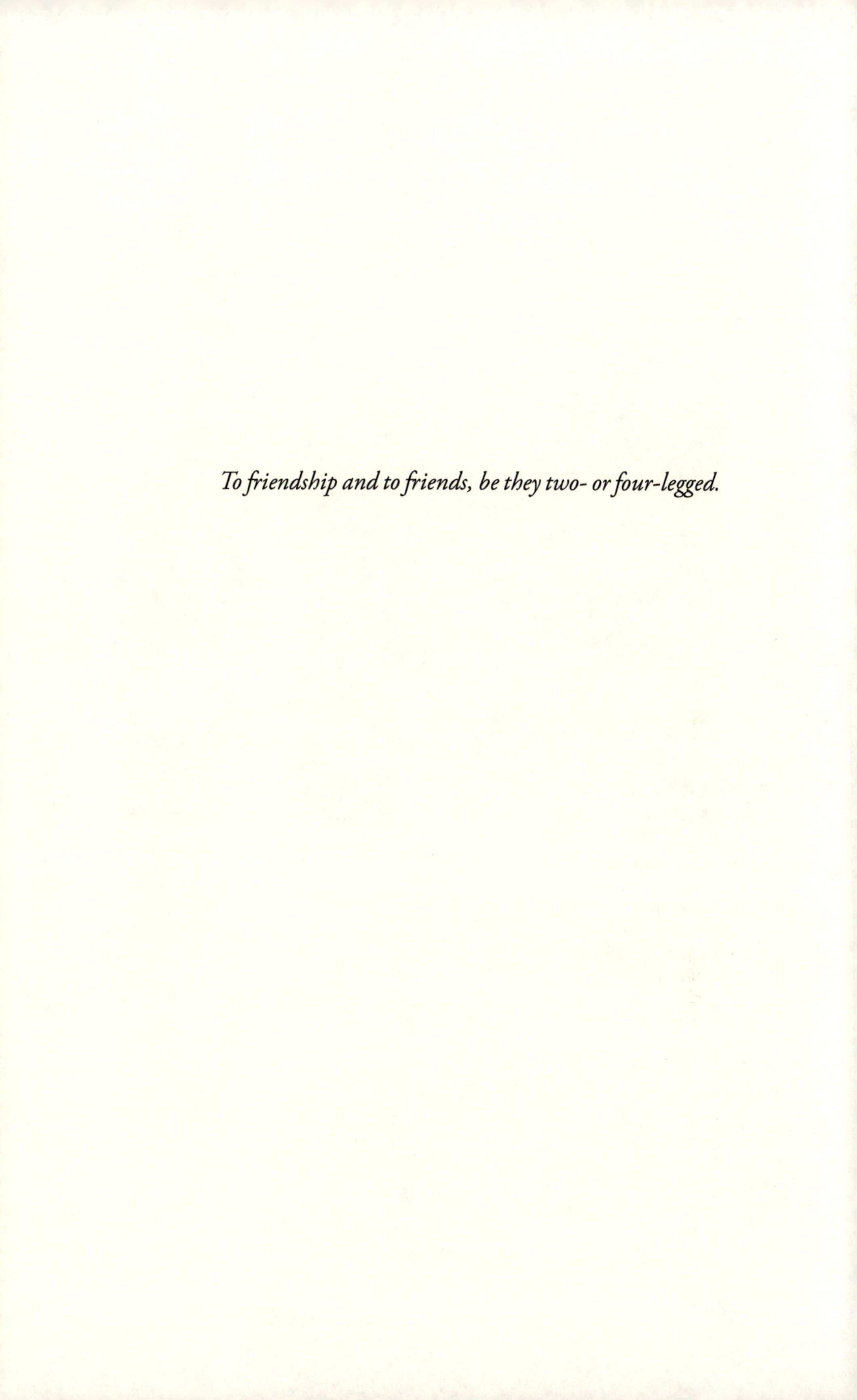

To friendship and to friends, be they two- or four-legged.

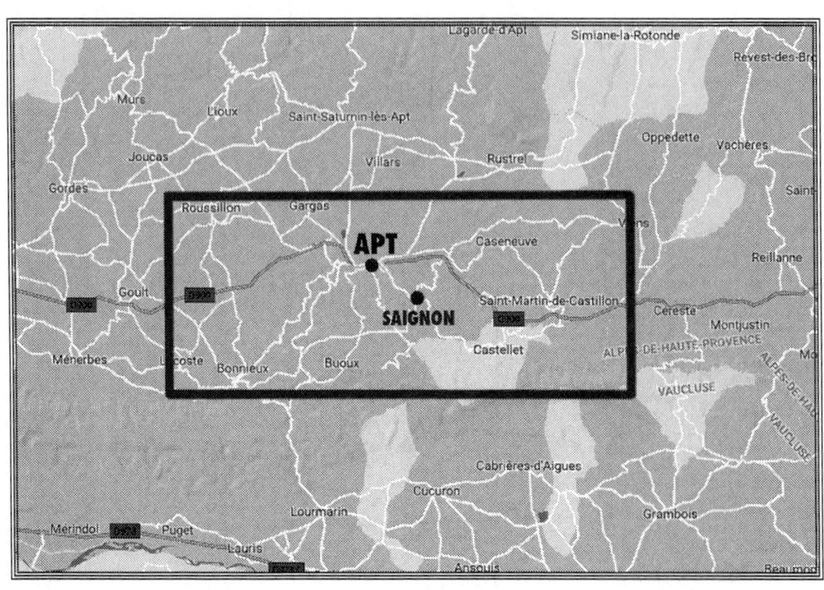

Lagarde-d'Apt
Simiane-la-Rotonde
Revest-des-Br
Murs
Lioux
Saint-Saturnin-lès-Apt
Oppedette
Vachères
Joucas
Villars
Rustrel
Saint
Gordes
Roussillon
Gargas
Caseneuve
Viens
Reillanne
APT
Goult
Saint-Martin-de-Castillon
Céreste
Montjustin
SAIGNON
Ménerbes
Lacoste
Bonnieux
Buoux
Castellet
ALPES-DE-HAUTE-PROVENCE
Mo
VAUCLUSE
VAUCLUSE
Cabrières-d'Aigues
Cucuron
Grambois
Mérindol
Puget
Lourmarin
Lauris
Ansouis
Beaumon

The ache for home lives in all of us, the safe place where we can go as we are and not be questioned. It impels mighty ambitions and dangerous capers.

— Maya Angelou

1 Winter Vacation

My Diary

Domaine des Claparèdes – Provence, Southern France

February 6, 2003

I am having a super time here. AND, I am so excited. I've been talking to Lizzie and Andrew, and I think it might work out for me to come and be the property guardian. All these years I've been teaching about France, and now I might actually be able to live here. Fingers crossed.

IT WAS THE DEAD OF WINTER, and I was vacationing at the *Domaine des Claparèdes.* The property was located outside a small village in Southern France, in an area known as the Luberon in the region of Provence.

The name of the village was Saignon (sometimes confused with the Vietnamese town of Saigon). Saignon is a *village perché,* literally perched atop a rocky promontory overlooking a deep valley and the town of Apt. Eight hundred years ago, it was a fortification, a lookout for danger riding toward Apt. At one time, Apt was the chief town of a Gallic tribe; it was destroyed by the Romans about 125 BC and restored by Julius Caesar. The plateau above Saignon was called the Claparèdes, meaning "rocky pile," ergo the name of my vacation spot.

The Domaine had once been an active lavender farm whose current owners were a British couple, Lizzie and Andrew, who now rented the lavender fields to a local farmer. They had converted the original farmhouse and all of the out buildings into vacation houses or, as they called them, cottages, and added two swimming pools.

I was staying in what had once been a small barn. The house had large door windows, and the Provençal sunlight flooded the rooms. Looking west, an enormous lavender field stretched toward Mt. Ventoux, looming on the horizon. I had visions of cyclists in the Tour de France, huffing and puffing their way to its summit. The lavender, known for its relaxing properties, bloomed in June and July when the plants exuded a sweet but not cloying aroma. Even in mid-winter, I could easily conjure up the fragrance. In the opposite direction, I saw low-lying hills of the Luberon range, and gazing up … the cerulean Provençal sky.

I had been invited to have supper with the owners of the property along with Paul, a fellow vacationer from England. Winter's evening darkness had descended as we got into my car. The rustic iron gates of the property creaked open slowly, and I turned the car a sharp left onto the macadam. The road followed a path originally made by farmers' wooden carts as their large wheels wound their way harvesting the lavender from fields on either side. The headlights showed a narrow, twisting, black thread of pavement, which we followed to the other side of the village.

"Turn here," Paul directed, as we rounded a sharp bend. I gingerly negotiated the turn where a signpost read *Clos de Lantins*. "This is it. Their house is called *Les Lantins*." I was reminded that in rural France, houses do not have house numbers; they have names. In a world full of technology and numbers, this throwback to simpler times appealed to me.

The lane ended abruptly, and a short driveway brought us into the front yard of an elongated bulky structure, all Provençal gray stones and contrasting red-tiled roof. Lights shone through large windows flanked with blue, wooden shutters.

The door flew open and there was Lizzie, her medium height and lithe swimmer's body silhouetted in the light. Cropped blond hair framed an almond face with sparkling, brown eyes.

"You made it. Come on in," she exclaimed with an exuberant, British accent.

We exited the car and followed her into the large kitchen-dining room combination, where Andrew was standing at the stove.

Andrew, an architect, had a tall, slender body, testimony to the hours he spent cycling and jogging the hills and lavender fields on the Claparèdes plateau above Saignon. He spoke with a faint British accent, and his brown eyes were smiling as he turned from his meal preparations, wiping his hands before extending them in welcome.

The story I learned that night was he met Lizzie when she crashed her bicycle into his. The image was charming to me then, but I would come to understand exactly how in character it was for her to crash a bike. Lizzie always seemed to go at full speed and often in different directions. The Brits have a word for it: "scatty."

Like most of the expats in the Luberon region of Provence, these two had come to escape the harsh weather of the U.K. They'd bought a run-down farmhouse bounded by a lavender field and a cherry orchard. Over the years, they'd added onto the house, which now was a sprawling property they'd named the Lantins. Several years later, they'd purchased the Domaine des Claparèdes on the opposite side of the village.

I'd bought a bouquet as a hostess gift, but getting the flowers unwrapped and inserted into water was no small task. Jet, the family's black Labrador, kept leaping at the bouquet. He seemed convinced the flowers were something intended for him, most likely something to assuage his Labrador appetite. "Jet, *non*! *Lâche*!"

The French equivalent of "drop it" seemed to have no effect, and I watched, amused, as Jet proceeded to grab the ribbon wrapped around my gift and run into the other room with it.

Looking up, I saw three pairs of eyes regarding our circus-like entrance. "Children, come here and say hello." One by one the children, boys, ages twelve and eleven, and a girl, eight, moved toward us, each extending a hand. Having performed their duty, they retreated to watch television in the family room.

Sipping glasses of wine, we conversed as Andrew prepared a first course of individual truffle soufflés. The prized subterranean fungus was plentiful in the area, IF you knew where to look, and Andrew had trained Jet to sniff them out. Traditionally, pigs were trained to hunt truffles, but it turned out to be easier to wrestle a prized truffle from a loyal dog than from a greedy pig. Lasagna, salad, a cheese board, vibrant conversation, and a lot of wine followed the soufflés.

Somewhere mid-meal Andrew made the announcement. "We're leaving France and moving to Australia." There was a moment of stunned silence as Paul and I absorbed the impact of his words. Further conversation revealed that Andrew's architectural specialty of historic restoration had earned him a job in Sydney, overseeing the renovation of an ancient Australian cathedral. He and Lizzie hoped to get their children enrolled in the International School there.

"What are you going to do about the rental cottages?" Paul asked. "Well," Lizzie replied, "we plan to get someone to move onto the property and act as a guardian. The guardian will have their own cottage, rent free, in return for taking care of things."

Someone?

And just like that, I was a little girl in the classroom, wildly waving her hand at the teacher, silently imploring, "Choose me! Choose me!"

I sat there with my mind spinning. Could this be my chance to stay in France? A year in Provence. My very own cottage. I thought about my native, cold, gray Michigan. Why did I need to stay there?

DURING THE REMAINDER OF MY STAY we talked, and in the end, Lizzie and Andrew offered me the job. A plan evolved for me to return the following summer and, when they left for Australia, I would take over care of the property. Not one of the three of us felt the need for written contracts. I was a mature, responsible adult. They were well-established members of the community and nice people. Why would we need something in writing? What could go wrong?

Before I left to come back to the States, Lizzie explained she had already taken reservations (or, as the British say, "bookings") for the following summer. The cottage assigned to be mine as guardian was already booked, as were the others. But I was not to worry, because she had arranged for me to stay in an apartment on the other side of the village from the Claparèdes. Not quite on-site accommodations; I would be temporarily housed with her friends, Meg and Stephen. I felt a tinge of disappointment but managed to tamp it down.

I was, however, curious and phoned the couple to see if it might be possible for me to take a look at the apartment. Lizzie gave me directions … down to the village, turn at the post office … continue past the abbey and on to a little hamlet with a sign *Les Gavots*. I managed to find the house, tucked back off the road sitting above a vineyard: an old Provençal farmhouse, nestled into the hillside.

Meg greeted me warmly. Her dark-brown eyes were set in a smiling, round face, topped with medium-brown hair. There was no mistaking her British roots as she extended her hand and spoke.

"Hello, Jo Anne. Let me take you down and show you the apartment."

We descended enormous stone slabs, which served as stairs to the lower level, where a former horse stable and tractor shed had been converted into two apartments now used as summer vacation rentals. Mine was absolutely perfect … the view was marvelous. Below the apartment terrace, a vineyard stretched toward the horizon, where the hills were dotted with more vineyards and fields of lavender. Beyond the fields, the Luberon mountain range rose skyward. Little did I know I would eventually spend many hours seated on that terrace feeling very comfortable and relaxed.

2 Stepping Back

FROM THE MOMENT I SET FOOT back in Michigan, I began making plans for my return to Saignon. Just a few months ago, I was at loose ends. It had been twelve years since I'd built my dream house in the small village of Glen Arbor, and this northern vacation spot on the shores of Lake Michigan had become my home. I can remember walking through the village and being overcome with a sense of belonging. It was as if I'd been destined to settle into this quiet spot. But, over time, my comfort level had declined.

After moving into my dream house, I'd acquired two cats. I'd adopted Beemer, a caramel and café au lait combination of colors, who was then one year old. His name wasn't short for the snazzy expensive automobile but an abbreviation of some exotic East Indian name given to him by his original owners.

My other cat, Snowflake, AKA, "Snowy," moved in two months after I'd adopted Beemer, and the vet thought he was a couple of years older. He looked just like the cartoon cat, Garfield, except Snowy was (ah hem) snow white. But his profile was pure Garfieldian, tipping the scales at fifteen pounds. Sometimes, when people met him for the first time, they'd call him Snowball. Beemer and Snowy had become best buddies, often sleeping curled around one another.

I'd majored in French at the University of Michigan and taught

French for most of my career. When I retired, I put my French books on the shelf but dabbled in writing for a company that published foreign language learning materials. The work, however, was sporadic, and I'd had enough of things educational. I hadn't been really unhappy, just twitchy. I kept trying to push the feeling to the back of my mind and be content with early retirement, but I couldn't. I was uneasy ... restless. I couldn't define it, this feeling of being restless. I loved my house, my pets ... Northern Michigan ... but my earlier feelings of belonging had weakened. It was as if I kept looking over the horizon, hoping to find something new and exciting.

I thought back to a summer night a year before, when I'd had no idea what was in store for me. I was having trouble falling asleep. I wasn't just nighttime restless, I was lifetime restless. I remember glancing at the clock: 2 a.m. Swinging my legs over the side of the bed, I shuffled to the kitchen.

What would it be? A cup of chamomile tea or a shot of whiskey? Unable to decide, I made the tea, dumped the whiskey into it, carried the cup of brew to the living room, and plopped down to think. I was about half asleep, my mind drifting, when I heard a voice.

"You know what you really need?"

Who said that? Where was the voice coming from? I tried to ignore the question, but after a couple of minutes of intense concentration, I spoke to the space ... . "Yes," I said, "What I really need is another life. I'm running out of years."

In my twenties, I'd tried marriage two and a half times. The first time was a flop, so I went back for a second opinion. The second time was worse. As for the half, let's just say I bailed before getting trapped by a man who was courting his investments and bank account instead of me. Not sexy.

There was an interval between marriage #1 and marriage #2 when, being restless even back then, I went searching. I took up yoga, only to discover my body was never intended to make itself pretzel-like. You've heard of the "days of wine and roses?" For me, it became the days of vodka and Valium, which didn't work either. I was still restless.

I'd scrapped my urban life in southern Michigan and moved "up north." People who live in Michigan, Indiana, Illinois, or Ohio know what it means when someone says they are going "up north" on vacation. The Northern Michigan area around Traverse City and the Sleeping Bear Dunes National Park have been dubbed "The Cape Cod of the North" and "The Riviera of the Midwest." This was where I'd vacationed as a young girl with my parents and younger brother, Joe. It boasted inland lakes, sand dunes, and miles of Lake Michigan shoreline. At the time, the area had seemed ideal—who says you can never go back? In my case, I'd decided on more than a vacation and had moved permanently (I thought) to Northern Michigan.

I'd relocated from big city to small village. I went from buying blackout shades for cutting the street light glare in my bedroom, to wearing a Mag-lite flashlight around my neck whenever I ventured more than a few steps from my house after dark. A change of scenery worked pretty well for a few years, but I became restless again.

I'd needed something new, and thanks to a local artist, I took up watercolor painting. I rented a small space in one of Glen Arbor's shopping areas and opened a gallery where I sold my own paintings, plus those of other artists from the region.

That's when my artist teacher invited me to join a group to go painting in the region of Provence, Southern France. Based in a tiny hamlet, we spent two glorious weeks painting the vineyards and surrounding villages. I loved the scenery and the serenity. The area exuded a real sense of history and permanence.

As a teacher, I had studied in Paris, but this was Southern France. This wasn't museums, the Eiffel Tower, and big city smog; this was fields of lavender, miles of vineyards, and an endless, azure-blue sky. After this sampling, I'd decided I would continue to follow the sun to Provence, and a year later, I organized my own group of artists to go to the area.

It was another successful trip, but the down side (if there was one) was that only some of us could be housed in the hamlet. Others had to stay in a small hotel in the village below. We ate meals and painted together, but then we'd go our separate ways. I really wanted to find a venue where we would all be together, not only for meals, but also for afternoon painting critiques and an evening's glass of wine.

It was then, via an internet search, that I'd found the Domaine des Claparèdes in Saignon. Early summer 2002, I visited the Domaine. The converted farmhouse and additional four houses meant everyone in our painting group could have either their own or a shared bedroom, bath, and kitchen facilities. It was perfect for a group of artists, and I reserved the entire property for the following spring.

I was intrigued with the setting and the ambiance and decided I'd do a preliminary visit for a few weeks the following winter. That winter stay led to my dinner with Paul, Andrew, and Lizzie, and my impending Provençal escapade.

AS I SPENT MORE TIME IN FRANCE, I would grow to appreciate the culture , the sense of history and the people. I felt as if Americans were interested in "things" … material possessions. America was all about newer, bigger, better, faster. To me, the French were interested in family, friends, and maintaining history. Particularly in Provence, life moved at a slower pace, and there was always time for conversation over a cup of coffee or a walk in the countryside. Life in France appealed to me. I wanted to have more of it, but my northern Michigan neighbor had trouble understanding.

"I'm moving to Provence," I announced.

She and I were having coffee together in the kitchen of my Glen Arbor home.

"Provence??" My neighbor gaped at me. "As in, Southern France?" I could practically hear her mind going around in a spiral: The retired teacher of French had finally gone over the edge.

"Not forever," I hastened to add, "Just for a year or two."

"But you just retired. You have a house and two cats. What are you going to do in Provence?"

She was staring.

I told her I was going to be the official on-site manager of five rental cottages on an old lavender farm. In France this is called being a *guardien* or, in my case a *guardienne*. In return, the owners were giving me my own stone cottage, rent-free. "They're off to Australia for a couple of years," I explained.

Still baffled, she asked, "But what will you have to do?"

"I'll have to meet and greet the guests and be sure the pool man, gardener, and housecleaners all do their jobs. Just think: Fields of lavender, the Luberon Mountains in the distance, and the sun shines 320 days a year."

Not bad, huh? was what I was thinking as I remembered endless winter days of Michigan gray skies. I could tell she wasn't convinced. She'd known me a long time, and had probably learned never to be entirely surprised when my life reached some imagined crossroads and took a hard left. After she walked back across the street to her own house, I imagined her saying to her husband, "Guess what Jo Anne is going to do *now*?"

I confess to having moments of doubt. Was I being realistic? I am what some people call a late bloomer. I do things out of order and have a tendency to learn life's lessons out of normal sequence. Lessons learned by most toddlers and teenagers, I waited to grasp until middle age. For example, when you're upset, eating lots of cookies and ice cream may make you feel better, but it can also make you fat, and you may throw up first.

Maybe I'm predestined to move in a kind of perpetual reverse. When I was in my late teens, people always guessed I was older than I was. And now, as *une femme d'un certain âge* (the French have such a nice way of labeling older women), I was continually told I looked much younger than my hard-earned years. I keep getting opportunities for change at a time when I should be rubbing my Social Security check like a magic lamp, waiting for the genie to pop out.

There at my kitchen table I played out the entire scenario in my mind … leave my home, my pets, and …

"Sit back! Stay put! Enjoy!" the imaginary voices urged.

"But I'm on the doorstep of Opportunity and Big Changes. My very own year in Provence," I answered back. Hadn't I already lived vicariously through Peter Mayle's tales of his moving to Provence in his books, *A Year In Provence* ... then *Encore Provence* ... and finally ... *Toujours Provence.* That could be it for me, too. A year in Provence.

"But you're retired," whispered the Voice of Doubt. "You finally have no demands on your time. No job to go to, no business to run. What the hell are you thinking! You can read, paint, write, walk, bike, dance, dream, garden, or NOT, just as you wish, right here in Michigan. Have you lost your mind?"

Suddenly I sat up, and for a moment I was terrified. I must have dozed off. Did I think I was twenty years old? That's when normal people did things like moving to France for a year.

When I was in my twenties, I was struggling with a new marriage, working hard at my first teaching job, juggling classes toward a Master's degree, and supporting my new husband who was in dental school. It was not a time of adventure for me; it was a time I tried to forget. Since those years, I'd had many opportunities to move on and do things differently—chances to re-create myself. Some I'd taken and, for the most part, those had turned out just fine. Some I hadn't taken and later wished I had.

I jumped up from the chair and, to no one in particular, I shouted, "Carpe diem! Seize the moment! Move over Peter Mayle, it's time for MY year in Provence."

3 Not So Fast

I TALKED TO MY BROTHER, JOE, and my sister-in-law, Sally, about my upcoming adventure. They'd moved to Glen Arbor a couple of years after I did, and Joe and I had grown very close. He was nine years younger than I and slightly taller than my 5-foot 7-inch height. He'd inherited our father's curly hair, which was now blondish gray, and sported a salt and pepper mustache and goatee.

Joe and I shared blond hair and steely blue eyes but distinctly different outlooks on life. Joe was a "glass half empty" kind of guy. I was (and am) the eternal optimist. His mind immediately jumped to the worst-case scenarios. What would I do if things broke down? How was I going to manage it on my own? Why would I want to take on all of that responsibility just to spend more time in France? To him, it made no sense.

Sally, several years younger than Joe, had a gorgeous head of medium-length light-brown hair streaked with blond. Her dark-brown eyes were set in an oval face with porcelain skin. The artist in Sally (and she was a good one) more easily saw the allure of my pending adventure. Eventually, they both got used to the idea and agreed to look after things on the home front. I was good to go.

I HAD LOVED LIVING IN GLEN ARBOR. Legally, it was so small it was not even an incorporated village. It just masqueraded as a village. It had a grocery store, a post office, a small bakery, a pizza restaurant, a bar, and a bookstore. Any major grocery shopping or things such as doctor appointments necessitated a twenty-five-mile drive to Traverse City and a twenty-five-mile drive back.

Joe and Sally weren't neighbors any longer, having purchased a house outside the village of Empire, some eight miles southwest of Glen Arbor, on the shores of Lake Michigan. I was tiring of the treks to Traverse City, and I'd been toying with the idea of selling my house for a year or so. Then, a fortuitous encounter with a friend gave me the impetus to put it on the market.

I'd gone into Traverse City one day to do a bit of shopping. Wandering the aisles of Office Max, I ran into a Leelanau County artist friend, Rod Conklin.

"Hi, Rod, how are you?"

"Doing great," he replied. "Really interesting I should run into you. You know how we've talked about how much easier life would be if we lived in Traverse City? Well, I've bought a condo."

I'm sure my jaw dropped a little, because Rod was a long-time resident of the more rural and secluded corners of Leelanau County. I knew he had begun to visit the Traverse City Senior Center regularly, and apparently, this had spurred him to think more seriously about moving to the town.

"Come on," he said, "If you've got time, I'll show you were it is."

We went to the parking lot, got in our cars, and I followed him across town. We entered a rutted alley just off a main thoroughfare. There, on one corner of a large, vacant area, was a house under construction.

"I thought you said it was a condo," I queried. I remembered the condominiums I'd looked at over the past couple of years. All had resembled apartment buildings in a big complex with common walls.

"It's what they call 'site condos'," he answered. "Let's the builder put more houses on smaller land space. Just a matter of zoning. There's going to be eight houses on the property, and they'll be called 'Woodmere Cottages.'"

I was intrigued. One thing I had not liked about the condos and apartments I had looked at was the common-wall thing. The buildings were often multi-storied, so you could have someone underneath your unit, or worse, overhead.

After more talk, Rod gave me the phone number of the builder, and I promised to investigate further. I met with the builder, and after reviewing the plans for Woodmere Cottages, more discussion, and some negotiations, I agreed to buy one of the condos yet to be built with the contingency I'd have to sell my Glen Arbor home first. In as much as the condos were under construction … not a problem.

When Joe and Sally had sold their Glen Arbor house, they'd had very good luck with a local realtor, Rob, so I phoned him. The next day he came to my house, and before you could say *"bonjour,"* I'd listed it for sale.

Maybe it was Fate; maybe it was the Universe guiding my life. I'll never know. But just three days later, I had a buyer for the house and at my asking price, too.

"You look stunned." Rob and I were seated at the counter in my house, and I was signing the purchase agreement.

"I am," I replied. "I cannot believe it."

"Well, there it is," he said, sliding a copy of the paperwork across the counter to me. The sale was finalized, and the buyers agreed I could stay in the house and pay rent until my condo was finished and I moved to Traverse City.

I began purging and packing. I sorted through cupboards and closets wondering how I'd ever accumulated so much stuff. I made frequent trips to the condo to meet with the carpenter, the electrician, and other workers as I put my own touches onto the builder's basic plan. I alternated from sadness at leaving a place that for a while had felt like home to the excitement of building a new one and the anticipated time in France. I began to feel much less restless, as if a goal were coming to fruition.

The condo was completed, and early in January, I prepared for my move. With boxes stacked around me, I looked out at the snow-covered ground and leafless trees. I'd had a good run here. I had enjoyed the wooded lot where I fed the birds, sat on my large deck, and meandered a short distance to the shores of Lake Michigan, but it was time for a change. I shook off sadness and focused on the new.

Early afternoon on moving day, the snow was falling. The movers arrived, and I watched with some degree of anguish as two young men loaded the last thirteen years of my life into the van. When it was all done, they headed out. I locked the front door and got into my car.

I didn't trust myself to look back. I needed to look to the future. I had six months to settle in to my new home before I would leave for France. Onward!

4 A New House

Woodmere Cottages, Traverse City

January 11, 2004

I'm in my new house. Even amid the chaos of moving, I love it. I shed a few tears as I turned off the lights in Glen Arbor for the last time, but I never looked back. The cats are adjusting gradually. Rod came over to say hi and visit. It'll be nice having him for a neighbor.

I SPENT THE NEXT SIX MONTHS settling the condo and preparing for France. Rod was a good neighbor and often came to chat over a cup of tea. He was tall and slim, had thinning, gray hair, a soft voice, and quiet demeanor. He'd been a full-time artist most of his life. Art galleries around the area sold his woodcarvings and paintings, but over the years, he'd stopped doing too much with his art and was enjoying retirement. We were the only residents at Woodmere Cottages that winter and watched together as the remaining units were built.

I was really attached to my cats and toyed with taking them along, but it wasn't practical. I ran an ad and found a house sitter, Christina, who would be the first of several such individuals. Added bonus: Christina loved cats.

Springtime morphed into summer, and the condo and cats were as settled as I'd get them. Christina moved in and, after final visits with Joe and Sally, I was ready to leave. The plan was I'd fly to Paris and take the high-speed train south to Avignon. Lizzie would meet me at the station. July arrived, and when it seemed like every tourist in the Midwest was on the way to my town in northern Michigan, I was leaving.

It had all started innocently enough. I went to look at a venue in France where I could take a group of artists. I ended up moving to a venue in France to experience life in France. Would this end up being my cure for restlessness? Would I finally feel like I was where I belonged?

5 The Adventure Begins

I STEPPED OFF THE TRAIN and onto the platform at the Avignon TGV Station. "*Je peux vous aider?*" It was a helping hand, as a Frenchman grabbed my bag and we headed toward the station. Entering, I looked around. Lizzie was due to meet me by the newspaper stand. Thanking the gentleman for his help, I scanned the waiting area.

No Lizzie.

Then, at the far end of the station, I saw her. With long, slim swimmer's legs and tousled, blond hair flying, she was running toward me and wildly waving her hand. Breathlessly she apologized. "I'm so sorry. There was an unexpected delivery at the house, and then I got caught in traffic."

I didn't know it at the time, but late, breathless, and perpetually besieged by the unexpected was Lizzie's default setting. Something with which I'd become painfully well acquainted. Over and over, I would be reminded of my Brit friends' word … scatty.

In the car on the way to Saignon, Lizzie explained I wouldn't be able to get right into my apartment at Meg and Stephen's. We were heading for a B&B, just down the road, where I'd spend a couple of days. I'd been shuffled to the apartment because my cottage was rented, and now I was being shuffled again. What could I say?

Approaching Saignon, we passed fields of lavender in full bloom.

Rolling down the car window, I inhaled the aroma. This was lavender land, and the sight and the scent were heavenly. I was in France among the fields of lavender! I could go to the open-air market in Apt on Saturday, and I could sit in the café and listen to the mellifluous sounds of the French language.

We turned off the highway onto a two-lane blacktop. Shortly, we passed under a large, iron gateway with the words "Chateau St. Quentin" in wrought-iron script overhead, and pulled into the grounds of a large, old chateau. Hauling my suitcase from the car, I was introduced to the welcoming hosts and shown my room. I looked around the room and at the grounds. Here was history. This old chateau, now restored, dated back to the seventeenth century. This is what I craved ... stability ... permanence. Compared to Michigan, this was OLD ... and I loved it.

My arrival, two weeks prior to Lizzie and Andrew's departure, had been timed to give us a period of orientation so I'd be fully up-to-speed on caring for the property. After a couple of nights at the Chateau, I moved into the apartment at Meg and Stephen's. The following morning, Lizzie picked me up, we met Andrew at the

Lantins, and my orientation started. There I was at the same house where just last winter the seeds of this adventure had been sown and fertilized with truffle soufflés, lasagna, and a lot of wine.

As my orientation started, they told me the Lantins would become another rental property, and I was to be in charge of it, as well as the small *cabanon* at the end of their cherry orchard. These two and the swimming pool were added to the five houses and two pools at the Claparèdes on the opposite side of Saignon. So now I had seven houses and three swimming pools to take care of in two different locations! This had not been a part of the original plan, but this is what I'd signed up for.

We left the Lantins and drove to the Claparèdes on the other side of the village, where it became apparent Andrew and Lizzie had differing views of my duties. Lizzie had said I'd oversee the pool man and the cleaning crew. Andrew began by showing me how to check the water level in the pool, and how to clean the BBQ grill.

That afternoon, we traversed the village back to the Lantins where Lizzie dashed in and out, sputtering bits of information about watching over the cleaning women. She kept telling me she'd make up a list of tasks, so I would know exactly what they were expected to do. A few days went by but no list appeared.

The rest of the day was a blur. I'd left my apartment at 8 a.m. and returned around 7:30 p.m. A high learning curve, plus the dashing from one side of Saignon to the other between the Lantins and the Claparèdes, had left me exhausted. I cooked some pasta, doused it with a jar of sauce, had a hot shower, and collapsed into bed. I had a few minutes before I nodded off. What in the hell have I gotten myself into? If there was an answer, I didn't hear it. I was asleep.

6 Reality

SOON AFTER I ARRIVED, I learned that the most compelling reason for Lizzie and Andrew to go to Australia—Andrew's job—was no longer that compelling. The proposed project of overseeing the restoration of the cathedral had evaporated. No explanations were offered, and it felt too intrusive and awkward to ask. It had seemed perfect, but somewhere between perfect and practical the plan broke down. Their relocation design was like the flight plan of an airplane; once filed and embarked upon, they'd reached the point of no return. Now the stated goal was to get their children into Sydney's International School.

The promise of my own cottage at the Domaine also had changed. The pre-arranged few weeks in the apartment with Meg and Stephen expanded to four months. It turned out that instead of reserving one of the cottages for me, as the guardian, Lizzie had continued to take bookings for them. Staying with Meg and Stephen was fine, except for the periodic necessity of moving out of one of their two apartments into the other, because the one assigned to me had been booked prior to Lizzie's arrangement with Meg. Lizzie had long known about these moves but chose to tell me later rather than sooner.

I became adept at transporting my belongings. There was one week—when both of Meg and Stephen's apartments had been booked—that Lizzie had arranged for me to move into the village of Saignon itself. I spent that week in a little third-floor studio apartment with no view and a narrow flight of twisty, old stairs to negotiate. I began to feel like a piece of furniture, being moved around to accommodate everyone except me. But I was in France. Lavender, markets, good wine, cafés …. Right!

Finally, Lizzie and Andrew left with the family, and I was in charge. Since I wasn't actually staying at the property, I needed transportation. So, Lizzie left me her minivan. Like 99.9 percent of the cars in France, it was a stick shift. After a few days, I developed the equivalent of tennis elbow. The frequent, necessary forays between my apartment and the Domaine properties on the opposite side of Saignon meant driving up the hill, around the curves, through the village, around the post office corner, and onward to the Claparèdes, necessitating frequent shifting. After Saturday guest arrivals, there were very few days when I did not have to go back to check on pools, meet a repairman, or respond to guest needs. But never mind, sore elbow or not I was in France. I had a free place to stay. As I drove past the lavender fields in bloom, I made it a point to inhale deeply. The aroma helped me calm down.

Lizzie had always insisted she would continue to handle the bookings from Australia. After all, there was phone, fax, and internet. However, her complete lack of, or often scattered, communication caused problems. More than once I was surprised with a last-minute message saying guests were due to arrive the next day, when none were on the schedule she'd given me for that week. How could I prepare for guests I didn't know were coming? These were not last-minute bookings on the part of vacationers; they were a matter of her disorganized and inefficient record keeping.

I had the credit card machine, and it was up to me to process the payments. Lizzie would send me credit card numbers and then phone with the final digits or necessary codes. Periodically, when the charge would be rejected, I'd find out the credit card company had mistakenly read Saigon (Vietnam) instead of Saignon (France). The mistake would have been amusing were it not for Lizzie's increasing expressions of stress over a lack of income.

The cottages were filled every week. Taking care of the Lantins and its pool and Cabanon on one side of the village along with five Claparèdes cottages, including the grounds and swimming pools, on the opposite side was daunting. Shortly after Lizzie and Andrew left, we had a broken window, a pulled-out pool gate, a non-functioning hot water heater, and a melted-down light fixture.

It wasn't long before Lizzie began to hint to me that Andrew might be coming back to France. She didn't say exactly when, why, or for how long. I thought it might be helpful to have him around to cope with some of the maintenance issues, but because the information had come from Lizzie, I didn't count on it happening. I'd begun to realize that when she was involved, things did not usually go according to plan. If in fact, there even was a plan.

August 8, 2004

30C and 78% humidity … another marathon 12 hours on Saturday. Lizzie called and I processed card payments. It was good to talk to her and I feel much better. She was appropriately gracious in her remarks about my handling of things here! A little positive feedback goes a long way.

A Brit couple left me a lovely bottle of wine and a very kind note. I do notice I'm getting better and better at the process and the heat. I've managed to dip in the pools a couple of times. Nice long dip as I left to come back here ….

Thank God, Andrew will be back in a few weeks and the picky repairs will be turned over to him. Just when it seems it's all running smoothly, something else comes up. Check on septic, BBQ not working, pool gate needs fixing, and on it goes.

CHANGEOVER SATURDAYS were especially chaotic. Guest departure was ten o'clock in the morning, and when they took their old sweet time departing, it meant a real scramble. We had to get beds changed, floors scrubbed, windows washed, and bathrooms tidy in time for afternoon arrivals. I wasn't just overseeing the gardener, the cleaning women, and the pool service; I was washing floors, doing laundry, and cleaning toilets.

Thank goodness for the hard-working housekeeping crew, headed up by Mireille. Her cropped, brown hair and snappy, dark eyes were a testament to her family's Moroccan origins. She was an equally indefatigable worker and talker.

She lived with her husband, Jean-Claude, and two sons in the village of Gargas, on the other side of Apt. Lizzie had alerted me to Mireille's characteristic chattiness, saying, "You'll just have to walk away from her, or she'll keep on talking." Many times, I did just that. Mireille didn't seem to be offended, and I put up with her talking because she worked diligently and we needed her. She and I often worked side by side after the other housecleaners had gone home. She eventually became a good friend, and her family became *ma famille française.*

In peak vacation season, all of the cottages were rented, and when there were late departures, the short changeover time created additional pressure and problems. I asked Lizzie about using a laundry service, but she wouldn't hear of it, saying it would be too expensive. After a few weeks of struggle, I made my case. Often, we could not get the cottages ready in time for new arrivals. It was not good PR to have guests arrive only to be told they'd have to cool their heels somewhere for a few hours while we finished preparing their cottage. Lizzie finally acquiesced, and we started sending the bedding to a laundry service. While this provided a partial solution, it also added work, because someone had to count sheets, duvet covers, and pillowcases, then fill out the laundry service forms, and reconcile the numbers when the items were returned. There was, inevitably, one less article in what came back than our records showed had gone out.

Mireille was stellar. She did the counting, prepared the forms, and checked in the laundered items. Soon, however, Lizzie demanded that I cut back on Mireille's hours. I was not to pay her for preparing and counting the laundry. Time was money, and money was tight. It only amounted to ten or twenty euros a week, but Lizzie had begun expressing panic about their lack of funds. I knew I couldn't manage without Mireille's help, so I kept her on the task and paid her out of my own pocket.

As had been hinted, Andrew returned from Australia a few months later. There were not enough clients in Australia who wanted his architectural skills full time, so he started commuting. He was in Southern France for a few months and then off to Australia to visit his wife and family. This was not a recipe for a happy marriage or a healthy family, and eventually things went sour. I was only slightly aware of this tension, however, since my communication with Lizzie focused on taking care of the properties.

Rumors began to surface saying Andrew had been spotted in a local restaurant cozied up to an unknown woman. I later realized how this factored into Lizzie's sometimes bizarre and even hurtful behavior toward me. She would praise my efforts and then turn around and criticize the way in which I'd handled Mireille's schedule. Dealing with her was like battling feathers in a stiff wind.

When her car needed a repair, she told me to take it to the local garage. While doing the repair, the technician said the car was overdue for an oil change, so I had them change the oil. Lizzie's response was to chastise me severely. How dare I spend money on an oil change!! I was confused, hurt, and angry. If I'd let the engine burn up, surely I would have been bawled out for not having the oil changed.

Even calling a plumber necessitated prior permission. So, should I let the water spew from a leaking pipe while I, in France, tried to contact her nine thousand miles and several time zones away in Australia? Our internet connection was the old dial-up mode, not always reliable, and it was at her discretion, not mine! Often, we'd arranged a time to communicate, but I couldn't make the internet connection work, and the eight-hour time difference made things infinitely more difficult.

I had all of the responsibility, none of the authority, and I was frustrated. But through it all, I kept repeating my mantra: I'm in France. I'm where I want to be (and some of the time doing what I wanted to do). I tried to focus on those things I craved: a slow pace of life, a sense of history all around me, and sunny skies so directly contrasting the gray ones of Northern Michigan.

August 15, 2004

It's HOT again. I'd hoped I was settling into a routine and tried not to be hard on myself. After all, a month wasn't a long time to learn the ropes of managing seven vacation houses (with pools and grounds and house-keepers to boot).

I'D BEEN SO EXCITED ABOUT SPENDING an extended time in France. I was loath to admit that maybe my brother, Joe, had been just a little more realistic than I. I had been pretty naïve in taking Lizzie and Andrew at their word about our agreement. Discussions the previous winter clearly had indicated the guardian—me—was to live on the property. The best, logical, and perfect choice for lodging was the cottage right next to the main gate off the road. I'd accepted the surprise of the extended stay at Meg and Stephen's, and even adjusted quite well to my week in the small apartment in the village. I was a little annoyed but too immersed in the tasks at hand to waste energy fussing about it.

I should have been in the cottage by the gate. But, at least I was in France. And it was definitely where I wanted to be. I relaxed into the culture of the country and the ambiance of the countryside. I was a world away from Traverse City's big cars, busy streets, and people in a perpetual state of hurry, hurry. Rural France was definitely more peaceful.

7 Taking Up Residence

IN OCTOBER, AFTER FOUR MONTHS in Meg and Stephen's apartment on the opposite side of the village, I moved to the Domaine des Claparèdes property. Lizzie had mentioned casually that for a while I'd be moving around among the different cottages. For a month I shuttled among them, depending upon which one had not been booked by paying guests. I got pretty adept at loading things into wicker baskets, which served as my portable dresser and closet. On the up side, it gave me hands-on experience living in the various cottages. I could speak knowingly with the guests about a sticky drawer in the kitchen or a pesky lock on a door.

As for that logical choice of the cottage next to the gate ... not quite. In retrospect, Lizzie was never going to give that one to the guardian. It was a larger house with two bedrooms and bathrooms. At no time was giving up that rental income a part of her plan. This was but one of many details that shifted betwixt plan and implementation, and never in my favor.

Finally, in late October 2004, I settled into the small cottage called *Le Potager*. A *potager* in French is a little vegetable and herb garden. This house was situated adjacent to such a garden and had probably been the equivalent of a glorified potting shed when Lizzie and Andrew bought the property. They'd enlarged the structure into a comfy, cozy, light, and pleasant little cottage. They'd added a fireplace in the combination living-dining room area, and I immediately had visions of winter evenings curled up with a good book in front of a crackling fire. My Glen Arbor and my Woodmere Cottage houses both had a fireplace, and I loved the ambiance and warmth of a glowing fire.

In autumn, with the major tourist season ending, there were fewer guests at the Domaine. Though it had taken several months, my time in France was finally beginning to approach what I'd imagined it would be. If there were no changeovers on Saturdays, I went to market in Apt and often joined Meg, Stephen, and a local ex-pat group for coffee.

Over the years, the Saturday market group had grown into something of a tradition among the ex-pat community. In the course of time, word had gone out … if you are English speaking and you want to meet up with others of like language, go to the Café Gregoire at Saturday market.

It was via my association with Meg and Stephen that I learned about this gathering and was welcomed "into the fold." As I assimilated into the ex-pat community, I began to look forward to that Saturday gathering. I loved being in France, among the French, but there was something comforting about that linguistic link to my native country.

Some of the ex-pats were summer-only residents, mostly South Africans. Others, like Meg, were from the U.K. and had sought the sunshine of Provence as a permanent home. There was a New Zealand nurse called Angel (whose real name was Karen) who lived in Saignon, as well as Lizzie's long-time friend, Henrietta, from Australia. The Saturday market café table was a potpourri of nationalities and personalities. But even in this ex-pat cocoon, I was surrounded by the mellifluous sounds of the French language and the sights of historical buildings. Oh, how I loved it!

I recall it was this time when I began to fantasize about France as "home." I felt more settled, I was making friends, and I really couldn't argue about the weather. I grew increasingly comfortable with daily life, as I learned more about local customs.

A Different Halloween

In the States, we make a big deal out of Halloween, but not in France. Halloween, after all, is the celebration of the eve of All Saints Day—All Hallows Eve. In most parts of the United States, All Saints Day gets lost in the candy corn shuffle, but not so in France.

All Saints Day is a national holiday in France, and it's traditional to put chrysanthemums on the graves of the departed. Huge displays of chrysanthemums for sale were set up in the supermarket and other parking lots in Apt, creating a patchwork quilt of brilliant yellow, bronze, purple, and white.

I didn't know why chrysanthemums were the flower chosen for this occasion. I did know if you are invited for dinner at a French home, it was customary to take candy, a small plant, or a bouquet of flowers. I also learned you never took chrysanthemums.

Drafts and Wind

I discovered the French had an absolute obsession with, and horror of, drafts and wind. French people rushed to close doors or windows whenever they perceived a draft—a *courant d'air*. Sitting in a draft caused all kinds of maladies.

The Luberon region of Southern France is a land of the maniacal *Mistral*. This wind starts from the North-Northwest, and gathers momentum howling and blowing southward down the Rhone River Valley. By the time it reaches the South, it is roaring. The Mistral can be icy, even in the middle of the summer, and is unrelenting. Absolutely nothing is safe in its path! It flips lawn furniture, slams doors and shutters, pushes pedestrians along the sidewalks, and causes normally obedient school children to misbehave.

Both *courants d'air* and the Mistral caused innumerable ailments (if you believed what you were told.) To ward them off, it was imperative to wear a scarf around your neck. Year round, neck scarves were everywhere on both men and women. It wasn't a fashion statement; it was a basic item of clothing.

One day, I braved the wind and made a quick trip to the closest supermarket. As I was about to enter, I noticed a frail, white-haired,

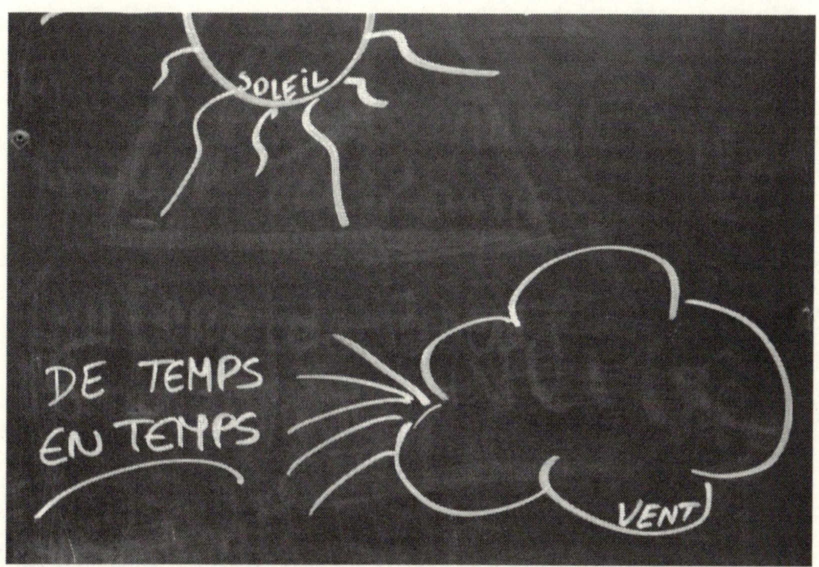

dark-skinned African man seated on the wall next to the entry. I'd often seen him there, scarf around his neck, reading a magazine, while his collection plate stood by, ready for offerings.

Walking into the store, I overheard a woman chiding him about sitting in a *courant d'air*, suggesting he move down the wall so he'd be more in the sun and less in the wind. Only in France would you hear a shopper giving advice to a beggar to get out of the draft.

Forming Friendships

It wasn't just learning about the culture and customs that added to my comfort level. I began making friends, and many of these friendships would continue well beyond my time at the Claparèdes. That first winter, Lizzie introduced me to a guest named Elizabeth, who was renting their Lantins house for the entire season and caring for Jet. I thought back to that Lantins dinner and Jet's mischievous attempts to pull the ribbon from the bouquet of flowers. Elizabeth, originally from Ireland, was slim, had medium-length, light-brown hair, and a ready smile to go with snappy, hazel eyes and a gentle manner. Lizzie had thought it would be good for Elizabeth and me to connect, both being single and on our own. Over the winter months, the two of us spent a lot of time together.

Elizabeth would sometimes bring Jet up to the Claparèdes; we'd wander along the edge of the lavender field while he searched for truffles under the nearby oak trees. I enjoyed her company, easy laughter, and her stories of growing up in Ireland. She talked of her experiences as a flight attendant on Air Lingus and shared her sadness over the loss of her husband seven years earlier. After she moved on from her winter at the Lantins, Elizabeth and I continued to enjoy each other's company.

Lizzie's arrangement for me to stay in Meg and Stephen's apartment was the start of added, enduring friendships. Stephen, an American, was in his late sixties, and Meg, born and raised in England, was fourteen years younger. He was tall and slender, and had been a runner and a tennis player in his younger days. His twinkling brown eyes looked straight through you, and a salt-and-pepper mustache and goatee adorned his smile. Stephen and I quickly formed a pact defending ourselves from the onslaught of criticism for the way we used the Queen's English. Meg often joked that there were often times when she had trouble "translating" Stephen's American phrases. She loved to tell the story of how Stephen had an accident with his car. When he got home, he kept repeating, "I totaled the car! I totaled the car," and she had no idea what he was talking about. "Totaling" a car was not a term used in British parlance.

Meg spoke beautiful French, having studied it in school and having been a Paris nanny in her younger days. It was a constant source of frustration to her that Stephen simply didn't grasp the language, nor did he seem inclined to try too hard at it. I think his attitude was, why bother, when Meg was there.

As these friendships formed and I met more people, I could feel myself being drawn into the vortex of life in France.

November 7, 2004

Yesterday I headed to market, did some shopping and joined the group at the Gregoire Café. I'm beginning to feel I have a circle of friends and acquaintances. Can I make a life for myself here?

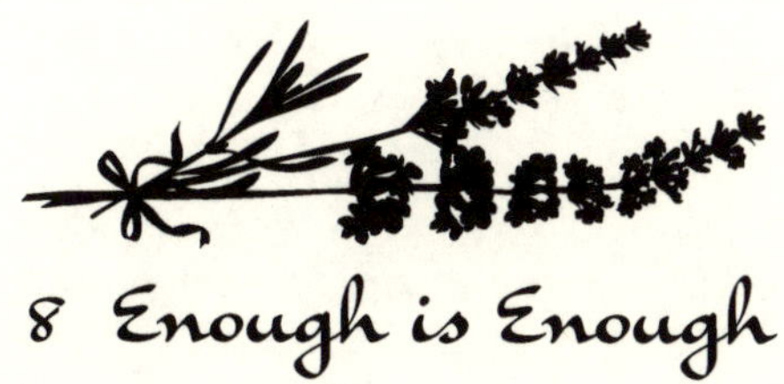

8 Enough is Enough

IN NOVEMBER, Andrew came back from Australia and took care of repairs, running credit cards, and Jet. Lizzie sent increasing numbers of emails complaining about the lack of renters, lack of money, and expressing concerns about the business. Finally, she ordered me to stop buying anything for the cottages, even cleaning supplies and toilet paper. She insisted we'd get by with what was on hand.

Her messages had intensified in frequency and tone of alarm just about the same time I'd caught hell over the car's oil change. After days and weeks of an emotional roller coaster, I decided I had to do something. I sent Lizzie an email and suggested that since Andrew would be in France for two months starting at the end of January, he could take over. I'd stay on, but as a paying guest. Lizzie accepted my proposal, and I'd have February and March to myself. Andrew was going to Australia in April, so that meant I'd be back "on duty," but I felt a real sense of relief. I could focus on being in France, markets, cafés, meeting friends, and more time to stroll the countryside. I could lie in my bed at night thinking how good it felt not to worry about what time I'd get up in the morning or what possible problem would crop up. It reminded me of those days when I first moved to Glen Arbor, and how peaceful it felt.

November 23, 2004

It's clear and sunny, but cold and frosty. Mireille is here cleaning one of the houses. More shit from Lizzie (will it never end?) I mentioned to her that I was thinking of writing a small book of essays called "Letters from Provence" about my time here. Lizzie panicked. She went on and on about what I can and cannot write about the Claparèdes. I'm stunned. What in the hell does she mean? What I can and cannot write? I've got to learn to keep my mouth shut and tell her NOTHING. I'd just like to feel some sense of stability and not the constant waiting for the other shoe to drop. Just when I think things have settled down, BOOM, another left hook. I did get some insight. Tax control, etc. In the end, she was her old, usual, chatty, chatty self. All sweetness and light. I do not trust her motives.

DESPITE THE UNEXPECTED MOVES, the communication difficulties, and the hard, physical work, one thing was certain … I was happy being here. I began to look beyond my time at the Claparèdes, thinking about where else I might stay. One of Meg and Stephen's two apartments could be an option, but I needed to explore the area a little more to be sure.

9 The Holidays

I WAS LOOKING FORWARD TO MY WINTER in Provence. Back in Northern Michigan, winters could be fierce, bitterly cold, and very, very gray. One of the attractions of Provence and the Luberon area was sunshine. It was said the sun shone 320 days a year. I'd have to see it to believe it, but I was willing to give it a go. My brief winter stay in 2003 surely had been a sunny one.

Years ago, I'd been diagnosed with S.A.D.—Seasonal Affective Disorder. Yep, no energy, wanted to sleep all the time … no oomph. With fewer guests at the Claparèdes, I was looking forward to taking long walks along the lavender fields and soaking up Provençal sunshine.

November 25, 2004 Thanksgiving Day

A year ago, I was preparing turkey with Joe and preparing to leave Glen Arbor and move to Traverse City with thoughts of what is NOW reality. I'm settled here in Provence!

THANKSGIVING CAME. Since the Pilgrims did not land in France, it's not a holiday there. I celebrated on my own by cooking a

turkey leg with some veggies. It was the first of many somewhat different Thanksgiving holidays I would spend in my adopted country.

November 30 was my birthday. The Borie cottage by the road was vacant, and Lizzie had given me permission to use it so I'd have room to invite Elizabeth, Meg, and Stephen for dinner. The cottage got its name from a miniature Borie in the yard. These beehive-shaped stone structures could be found all over the Vaucluse, and there were a lot of them on the Claparèdes plateau. They were stone-on-stone construction, usually just one small room. Mostly shepherds had used them, and more recently, hunters. The sight of these structures scattered around the countryside was another picture that I grew to love. They were mystical, magical, and a bit mysterious.

In preparation for my birthday dinner, I went to Apt, where I picked up made-to-order lasagna from the superb Italian deli. I also bought salad, and cheeses for a cheese board and, at the bakery, my favorite dessert … lemon meringue pie. I stopped at the local wine shop, V Comme Vin, where I purchased several bottles of my favorite wine, which was a mellow red from Constantin Chevalier, a vineyard a few miles south of Saignon.

That evening my guests arrived, and after a pre-dinner *apéritif* of a bubbly wine and local black olives, we gathered at the table. We enjoyed the food, wine, and vibrant conversation.

"Stephen, can I get you another serving of lasagna."

"No thanks, Jo Anne," came his quick reply, as he dabbed some crumbs from his mustache and goatee. "I saw that lemon meringue pie, and I'm saving room."

No one else wanted seconds, so it was on to dessert. They joined in singing "Happy Birthday to You," which brought tears to my eyes. I was celebrating my birthday in France! With new friends! I felt pretty darn happy, and my desire to stay grew. I wanted more birthday celebrations in France.

As I tried to analyze it, I think I longed for a feeling of belonging … that I was finally where I was supposed to be. I had experienced some of that feeling after moving to Glen Arbor. Over the years, any sense of real permanence always faded with time. Was there any such thing? I know they say that change is constant and inevitable, but I thought surely there must be stability and belonging out there somewhere.

10 Cars and Cats

ONCE LIZZIE AND ANDREW LEFT, I used her mini-van. As their income slowed to a trickle, they decided to sell her car. A friend of theirs had a car for sale: an older Renault Twingo. Andrew and Lizzie decided to sell her van and buy the Twingo. They proposed I use the Twingo for free but pay for the insurance and gas. Renault had named the car by combining the words "twist," "swing," and "tango." This one was bright red. I had to smile. The name definitely described the way I felt my life was going at the time.

Winter approached, and there were no guests at the Domaine des Claparèdes. It was empty but not lonely. Since my first stay, I'd enjoyed the peacefulness of the Domaine and its country setting. For me, there was a real difference between solitude and loneliness. Often, on a wintry night, I'd step into the courtyard and look at the twinkling zillions of stars above, and below the plateau, the twinkling lights of Apt. I was not lonely. Besides, there were always the cats for company. I'd left my own cat friends back in Traverse City in the care of my house sitter, Christina, but once in France had gained the company of the cats of the Domaine.

The cats were a motley crew. There was the queen, aptly named Sheba, who was a small tabby. Lizzie said before Sheba had been spayed she'd given birth to a number of the other feline residents. A large, male tabby named Freddy was head honcho. There was a

calico named Chloe, a smaller, all-white male they'd dubbed Henri, and a black-and-white female named Bianca. Only Sheba and Freddy showed any inclination of wanting to associate with humans and spent a lot of time in my little cottage. The vacationers also quickly accommodated their desire to be inside, but when renters left, the cats gravitated back to me. The others blithely went their feline ways but always managed to appear in the courtyard when dinner was dispensed.

I had ample time to explore the many walking and hiking trails that crisscrossed the Claparèdes plateau. This was one of the many things I'd grown to love about rural France. Open fields, nature, mountains in the distance, and the sprawling lavender fields. One of my walks, which I'd dubbed "The Loop," was a forty-minute jaunt from the Domaine toward the village of Saignon and back. A portion of this walk followed the same narrow, blacktop road winding among the lavender fields where I'd so carefully guided my car to that supper at the Lantins.

Often, I walked first thing in the morning when the sky was blue, the sun just appearing, and the courtyard grass frosty. I'd head across the courtyard and listen to my feet make crunching sounds on the icy grass. As the antique iron gate creaked shut behind me, I'd step east onto the macadam, letting my body absorb the warmth of the sun rising over the *Mourre Negre*, Black Mountain, which was the highest point in the Luberon chain. Often the tops of the hills were lightly dusted in snow, and as the sun crawled slowly over the crests, bathing them in a golden glow, it reminded me of honey being poured over a bowl of warm oatmeal.

By mid-winter in Michigan, the maples and birch trees would be stripped of their leaves. Only the pine trees provided any color, with their evergreen presences dotting the snow-covered landscape. Here, even in mid-winter, the leaves of the lavender plants showed a hint of purple. The rounded tops of the small bushes, symmetrically shorn by the harvesting machine, were ready to spring back to life. I'd close my eyes, imagining the scent of lavender in the air.

One morning, I was absorbed in my thoughts when I became aware of a large white shape coming into view, and with it a faint clink, clank, clink sound. As the shape and sounds came closer, I realized it was Francesca, a Great White Pyrenees, who frequently left her farm in a nearby hamlet to visit neighboring houses. The dog wore a small cowbell on her collar. I was never sure if the bell was to enable the owners to find her or to warn others of her presence. She wore a tag admonishing anyone who might be so tempted that she was not to be fed or taken in: *Pas de lit, pas de petit déjeuner, je pars!*—No bed, no breakfast, I'm leaving!

Lumbering up to me, she paused so I could pet her, scratch her furry ears, and talk to her. She joined me for a short distance, but after a while, realizing I had no treats, she ambled off across the fields.

11 Christmas

AS THE HOLIDAYS APPROACHED, I missed Joe and Sally more than usual. I enjoyed being in France and had begun to really feel at home, but friends are not the same as family. Then, I had a brainstorm. Why not have Joe and Sally fly over to visit me for the Christmas holiday? There would be fewer guests, and they could stay in one of the houses. I called them, suggested it, and happily they agreed. I had enough air miles to partially pay for their tickets, so the trip would be my Christmas present to them. I was very excited as I began to anticipate their visit!

We had no snow, but there was a heavy frost each night. In the morning, as I looked across the lavender fields, I imagined a white Christmas.

There might have been no snow, but myriads of white lights appeared, strung all over Apt: around lampposts, trees, storefronts, and houses. It was beautiful and magical. The Blachère Company, which produced decorative Christmas lighting for many cities all over the world, was located in Apt. This meant the holiday lights and decorations in Apt were Paris hand-me-downs from the previous year. All of the main town squares were surrounded by enormous, plain trees, but at Christmas they were wrapped and strung with millions of tiny, white lights, which would glitter and glimmer, shimmer and shine.

Apt was not a particularly pretty town. It was old and worn but authentic, and that's what I loved about it: it existed for the people who lived and worked there and not solely for the tourists. The town dated to Roman times, and in some sections the streets were made of cobbles, which were so worn it didn't take much to imagine Roman soldiers trooping over them. At Christmastime, however, the old and worn disappeared behind the swaths of white lights.

One of my favorite places was the Roman arch near the Cathedral of St. Anne, established in the twelfth century. At Christmas, it dripped with multiple strings of tiny lights cascading like waterfalls. Mesmerizing!

Christmas meant lights, and also chocolate. Imagine the longest aisle in any big supermarket completely filled on both sides with nothing but bars, bags, and boxes of CHOCOLATE! Apt had one of the most famous chocolatiers in all of France, and the *Bonbonnière* shop served an unbelievable assortment of candies. French chocolate is of a very high quality and gives new meaning to the phrase "melt in your mouth." Mostly dark and glistening, it is both satisfying and addictive.

In addition to chocolate, the shop windows, market stalls, and the supermarket displays were full of candied fruit. When writing to my friends about the fruit, I could almost hear the chorus of, "Blech, Yuk, Ich … candied fruit!" Most were thinking of those bilious red and green candied cherries grandma put in her fruitcake. This was not the same entity. Apt was the largest producer of crystallized fruit in the world, and the factory was a major employer in the area. Legend had it that these sweet delicacies were offered to the Avignon popes as long ago as the fourteenth century and earned Apt's delicacies a label of high quality and remarkable taste. My favorite was candied orange rind dipped in chocolate.

I couldn't wait to share the lights, chocolate, and my favorite fruit treats with Joe and Sally. I'd arranged with Lizzie to pay minimal rent for the Vue de Ventoux, across the courtyard from my *Potager* cottage. I remembered my first winter stay in the house with its view of Mt. Ventoux. I just knew Joe and Sally would be thrilled. The three of us had seen it on TV years ago as we watched the Tour de

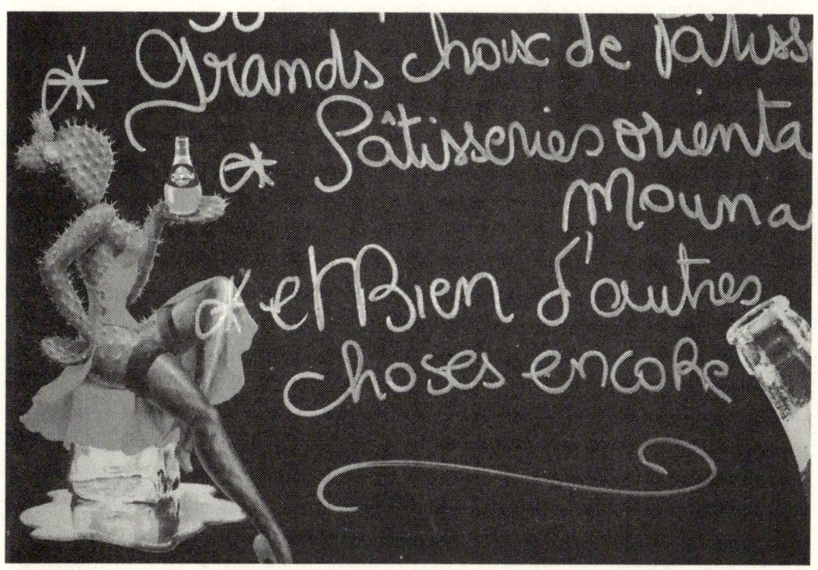

France together. Now they would be able to look at it in person! It was going to be so great to share Christmas with my family.

Sally was a teacher and Joe drove a school bus, so they were tied to school schedules with limited vacation time. Joe wasn't particularly fond of flying, and this would be a quick trip. Luckily, I was able to get business class seats on the overnight flight from Detroit to Paris. I knew from experience the comfort of business class could make a huge difference in one's level of fatigue and jet lag.

They would fly into Paris and take the high-speed train, the TGV, to Avignon just as I had months before.

I decorated the cottage with ornaments and put up a little Christmas tree. I loaded the refrigerator with special beers … Joe being more of a beer than a wine drinker. I could almost see his clear, blue eyes light up when he saw the variety of brews. I bought snacks, several bottles of nice wine (for Sally and me), and hauled in firewood so the fireplace was ready at the striking of a match.

They were to arrive on Monday, December 23. On Sunday, I went to the *marché paysan* in the nearby town of Coustellet for last-minute gifts and fresh produce. Thinking it was time for a break, I ducked into a little pizza restaurant for a bite of lunch and cup of coffee.

I was just finishing lunch when my mobile phone rang. The caller ID was one I didn't recognize, and when I answered, I was surprised to hear Joe's voice. There were no preliminary greetings or niceties.

"We're not coming," he said, "I just can't do it."

I was stunned and speechless. They'd driven from Glen Arbor south to Ann Arbor the day before, left their dog in the care of friends, and went on to stay that night at a hotel near the Detroit airport, to be close in case of wintry Michigan roads.

I've never known exactly what happened; Joe just said, "I can't." No one volunteered more of an explanation to me, nor did I have the courage to ask. I knew that Joe was prone to panic attacks, and I was left to surmise maybe he'd suffered a bad one.

I paid for my coffee and went back to my car. On the half-hour drive from the market to Saignon, I was in a daze. Here I was, living a dream, with an opportunity to share the experience with my family, and they had turned it down. In my heart, I knew they would never do anything to deliberately hurt me, but I was devastated.

December 23, 2004

The sadness hit me as each time I looked at the clock, I was reminded that Joe and Sally should have been at a given point in their journey. And then to see La Vue dark when it should have been lit up preparing for their arrival.

MY FRIENDS RALLIED 'ROUND. Meg called and invited me for lunch. Mireille came to visit the morning of Christmas Eve and brought me a lovely homemade *bûche de Noël*, a traditional French cake, made in the shape of a Yule log.

An Australian brother and sister, who were staying in the Borie, invited me to join them on Christmas Day. We had roast chicken and trimmings, a pleasant afternoon, and I did my best to focus on good food and the companionship. I made it through the day, but it took several days to muster the energy to undo the preparations I had so carefully arranged for Joe and Sally's visit. I shed more than a few tears over the whole episode, but eventually my disappointment dimmed.

Although there were very few guests, I checked the houses regularly and fed the cats. Lizzie continued to complain about the lack of money. At times, she acted as if she were doing me an enormous favor by letting me stay, instead of thanking me for all the work I'd done and was continuing to do. I tried to discount her histrionics, but her attitude was hurtful. I was taking care of their business as if it were my own, and feeling very unappreciated. I had only January to go, and then Andrew would take over. I would be on vacation.

12 A Guest

AS ANTICIPATED WHEN HE RETURNED, Andrew stepped in to manage things, with the help of Lizzie's French friend, Joelle. Joelle was tall, slender, had short, dark hair, a deep voice, a warm smile, and pleasant manner. She had retired as an art teacher from the school in Apt. She was friendly and approachable, and as time went on would become another link in the chain of events I experienced in ensuing years.

My agreement with Lizzie in place, I stayed on as a paying guest. Over the next couple of months, I have to confess it was with no small amount of smugness that I observed things go awry … and needed to do nothing but watch. Towels left on the line for days and a broken shutter swinging in the wind. Not my problem! I did, however, still feed the cats. No need for them to suffer neglect.

Once free of the guardian obligations, I had more time to enjoy markets. On market day in Apt, I'd wander the stalls and listen to the loud calls of the various merchants as they'd hawk their wares. There was a friendly competition among them as well as camaraderie. One morning, I went early and settled in at the Cafe Gregoire to wait for Meg, who was joining me for coffee. As I got comfortable with my International Herald Tribune and ordered my *grand crème* (that's a big cup of coffee with warm and foamy cream), I noted a long table being cleared of empty wine bottles, bags of crumbs of baguette and croissant, as well as evidence of coffee and juice and sandwiches. As I watched the occupants clearing up their debris, I realized they were all vendors from the various stalls around the square. After a fleeting thought about how scandalous it was that they should be drinking and eating so heartily at 9 a.m., I realized these people had probably been up since 3 or 4 a.m. to drive to Apt and then set up their stalls. This was not breakfast! This was their lunch!

As I prepared to go back to Michigan in the spring of 2005, I realized how much I wanted to stay. I couldn't do that, of course, but I began to think how great it would be to come back to the Luberon next winter. Provence was not done with me. Oh no! She had me by the nose … lavender and all. I wanted, no, *needed* to come back. I needed to spend more time in the Luberon, to continue to see my friends, to go to market and walk the hillsides with Meg and the group. I continued to fantasize about living there. Could I perhaps, move there?

You would think I'd had enough of the Domaine des Claparèdes, but minus the obligations, and the frustrations that had gone along with them, I loved it. Maybe it was a question of better the devil you know, but I decided I wanted a return stay at the Domaine. This necessitated making arrangements with Lizzie.

February 6, 2005

I'm in a muddle over the rental for next winter. I wrote to Lizzie about which cottage might be available but no reply.

Hopefully, she's just taking time to process and do some numbers.

WHEN LIZZIE FINALLY DID REPLY, she made references to possible part-time caretaking. Did I want to walk down that road for a second time? I worried about what it was going to cost me to come for the winter. I knew the ropes, and I'd be there anyway, and it would not be full time. Why not? But the proverbial devil was, indeed, in the details, and I knew from experience details were not Lizzie's strong point.

I wanted to rent the Vue de Ventoux, the house where I'd spent my first winter vacation. The views beyond the lavender field toward Mt. Ventoux were stunning, and the house sunny and spacious. Ultimately, I negotiated a good rate and agreed there might be periodic caretaking to offset my expenses. Lizzie even lowered the price just a little when I said I'd feed the cats. I was set, but wise enough to ask Lizzie to send me a contract or letter of agreement, so all would be in writing. I'd learned that lesson.

April 4, 2005

Andrew is gone. Lizzie is sending crazy emails, micromanaging the cleaning ladies. Then she screwed up the names of the people arriving tomorrow. No response to my request for a contract for next winter.

AFTER ANDREW LEFT, I was back to checking the pools, closing the front gate, feeding the cats, and prepping for incoming guests. When there was no one in the Lantins house on the other side of the village, I trekked over there, checked the grounds, and ensured the alarm was set.

As much as I felt sad getting ready to leave, I felt good knowing I'd be coming back. Mireille and Jean-Claude would keep my suitcases with clothes, so I didn't have much to transport back to the States. It felt pretty darn good to think of my belongings waiting for me there, in France.

Things went well and at the end of April, when Andrew came back, I happily turned the properties over to him. I left France with plans already in place for my return in October. It was time to get my head and my heart turned around to my life in Traverse City.

May 1, 2005

It's time to leave. A roil of emotions. Mireille came to drive me to the TGV in Avignon. I cried, Mireille cried. As we drove out of the gates, I realized how attached I'd become to the Claparèdes and France.

13 Changes

May 29, 2005

Back in Traverse City, but really mixed feelings. Thinking about springtime in the Luberon. Sigh.

HOUSE SITTER CHRISTINA HAD MOVED OUT, and I embarked on a summer of getting better acquainted with my Woodmere Cottages co-owners. Dear neighbor Rod and I had fun comparing notes over how things had progressed since that first winter, when he and I were the only occupants. Now there were eight households. He hadn't sold the family farm in Benzie County and spent a lot of time there. When he was around, he joined me and the other residents for group picnics. Sometimes he'd settle his long frame into a porch chair and visit or join in an impromptu evening resident-gathering.

In spite of these contacts, I didn't feel the same sense of ease with my Michigan neighbors as I felt with my friends and acquaintances in France. Sometimes when we were sitting on the porch, I'd gaze at the stars and realize my mind was miles away, thinking about the stars over the Claparèdes.

The neighbors mostly were agreeable, but others proved to be difficult. One of the most difficult was my next-door neighbor, Peggy. She was diminutive, had short, curly, dark hair, and was one of those individuals I classified as perpetually perky ... a characterization I did not mean as a compliment. She was an elementary music teacher, which may have accounted for her constant beaming smile and chirping, high-pitched voice. I was sure kids loved her. She'd drop in unannounced and seemed to have no sense of personal space or the meaning of privacy. She was nice enough, but her constant chatter and bubbling personality wore me out. If I were going to go to work in my little garden, or just relax on the porch, I'd peer out first to see if she were anywhere in sight.

Joe, Sally, and I struggled with how to handle the aftermath of their aborted trip to France. They found out the trip insurance would not cover anything. The best I could figure out from their explanation was, if it had been a panic attack, Joe had waited too long to go to the doctor, which nullified the insurance. Eventually they offered to pay me some money, and we worked out a satisfactory solution for payment. I accepted some money; but it wasn't the money that mattered, it was my badly bruised feelings.

I didn't like feeling estranged from them. We'd grown very close when they'd lived in Glen Arbor. After they'd moved to the village of Empire and I'd relocated to Traverse City, I'd frequently travel the twenty-five miles to spend the day at their place in the country. They were my real family, and I wanted to feel close to them.

It took some time and frequent visits, but gradually we got past the unpleasant memory. By the end of the summer, the aborted trip to France was no longer the elephant in the room.

I tried to fit back into my stateside life, but my head and my heart were back in the Luberon. I couldn't help thinking of sitting in the sun at *Chez Christine* in Saignon, with my coffee and croissant and talking with Meg ... or wandering the streets of the village and looking up at the clock tower, which dated to 1584. I missed that calm relaxation and sense of longevity. Life in the States felt superficial, shallow, full of supersize and speed.

I chatted with neighbors, visited Joe and Sally, and thought constantly about lavender (which would now be in full bloom) and Provençal blue skies. House sitter Christina was gone, so I needed to find a replacement for the upcoming winter.

Ad: *The Traverse City Record Eagle*

Wanted. House and cat sitter. Mature, responsible individual to occupy my home and care for two cats while I travel. Pay utilities only. Must provide references. 231-323-6785

THE DAY AFTER MY AD APPEARED, a young woman answered it. Melissa had just finished her PhD and was setting up practice as a psychological counselor in Traverse City. She was trying to get on her feet financially, and moving to my condo for housesitting would mean she'd save money over renting or buying. Melissa was medium height, slender, had long, brown hair and hazel eyes, and spoke with a soft but clear voice. She also had a bubbling laugh, and her demeanor left me with no doubt she was going be a very successful therapist. We hit it off immediately and agreed she would take over care of my condo and the cats when I went back to France.

For the next three years, Melissa stayed on as my housemate in the summer and oversaw condo and cats when I left for France in the fall. Eventually, she bought her own house, but we continued our friendship. She took Beemer and Snowy when I was in France and brought them back to me in the spring. I often said she was a cross between a best friend and the daughter I never had.

As October weather turned autumnal, I cleaned and cleared closets getting ready to turn all over to Melissa. Chilly, blustery weather indicated I was leaving at just the right time. Late October often brought the first snow to Northern Michigan, and I had no desire to see it.

14 A Car

WHEN I'D PARTED COMPANY with Andrew and Lizzie, I'd also parted company with the Twingo. I needed a car in France. Most major car rental companies offered an extended rental option for people staying several months. Then, I got an email from Meg saying a friend in France wanted to sell her car. Would I be interested in buying it?

Meg's friend, an American from California, had decided she wanted a smaller vehicle. (I should have taken the hint.) I trusted Meg, and after a quick consultation with my financial advisor, I said, "Yes." This only added to my excitement and anticipation. I was going to have my very own car in France; it was feeling more and more like I lived there and not in Michigan.

Late October Melissa took me to Cherry Capital Airport. Arriving in Paris at Charles de Gaulle, I felt like an old hand as I made my way through immigration and on to baggage claim and customs. I trekked the length of the terminal to the TGV station and the last leg of the journey.

The high-speed train headed south to the TGV station in Avignon, and during the three-hour-plus journey rooftops gradually shifted from austere northern gray to Provençal red tile. As villages zoomed past, I glimpsed the always-present church steeple poking skyward, and experienced an overwhelming feeling of warmth and familiarity.

"JO ANNE, JO ANNE ICI!" It was Mireille on the platform of the train station waving her hands at me. Brown eyes teary, she threw her arms around me and, abandoning the customary French kiss on each cheek, gave me a long and resounding big one.

"Ah, ma Mireille, *quelle plaisir de te voir*," I replied, hugging her in return. And it truly was a pleasure seeing her familiar face.

"*Jean-Claude nous attend dans la voiture*," she announced, and grabbing my suitcase, we headed to where her husband was waiting in the car. We made the forty-five-minute drive back toward Apt, stopping at their house in Gargas where we loaded my things they'd stored, and drove on to the Domaine des Claparèdes in Saignon. They left me in the Vue de Ventoux house where I'd first stayed. It felt familiar and comfortable.

October 24, 2005

It feels so good to be here. I'm unpacking. Meg came and picked me up. I visited with her and Stephen, had lunch, and got the car. It's bigger than I had envisioned, but it'll do. Sheba and Freddy are both in the house. In a way, it seems odd not to be in charge.

THE FOLLOWING WEEK, I negotiated the paper work for the car and became the proud owner of a 1997 Toyota Carina. It was a big four-door, dark-gray sedan, perfect for getting around. I was so excited. If you owned a car, didn't that mean you belonged?

For years back in the States, I'd always had nice cars. There was a time when I wouldn't have been seen in anything but the latest, biggest, and the best. I fondly remember my big Buick Riviera … two-toned brown and oh so sleek. That was followed by a four-door Buick Electra 225, dark blue and sophisticated.

Being in France allowed me to step into a new persona. No longer Jo Anne of the sleek, modern, big car. I was now French Jo Anne …

scoffing at the typical American notion that bigger is better. French Jo Anne would choose an older vehicle, or a tiny little gas-saving model, or a combo of both. I opted for older. Turns out it was actually quite big.

Ten years later, I still had the car. I'd dubbed her "The Old Gray Mare." She soon boasted over 200,000 kilometers of distance traveled. Each year, I talked about getting rid of her and getting something smaller. Parking a big four-door family car in any French town was a challenge. I'd pull into parking lots only to realize my bulky gray mare would not fit into any of the stables.

But I gradually got the hang of driving the Carina. Yes, she was big, and yes, she was old, but it was MY car. I decided I would drive her until she dropped. Maybe then I could sell her for parts. They shoot horses, don't they?

IT SEEMED STRANGE to be at the Claparèdes as a paying guest, yet it felt familiar. Freddy and Sheba quickly resumed their customary habit of shuttling in and out. Their feline presence added to my sense of comfort.

While Andrew was coming and going between France and Australia, Lizzie's friend Joelle was taking care of the property. In addition to looking after the cottages, Joelle worked on the grounds and the gardens as much as she could; however, once I took a good look, I could see that the absence of owners was disturbingly apparent. The herb garden/*potager* next to the little cottage where I'd lived a year ago was overrun with weeds, and paint was peeling off shutters. Joelle openly expressed her concern about the state of things, and there was a lot I could have said, but I just listened.

October 31, 2005

I had a long talk with Mireille. Things are not good with Lizzie. Joelle brought up a sweet old desk for me to use. She is not happy. I'm settling in and slowing down. It's a different pace of life entirely, and no matter how often I come, it's an adjustment. I'm learning all over again how to relax.

I RE-ENTERED MY LIFE in the Luberon but with periods of questioning. Where did I really fit in? I'd often sit and gaze at Mt. Ventoux, wondering. I'd been chasing the idyllic life, and crossing oceans in my attempt to find it. I was where I'd thought I wanted to be, but I was beginning to face the reality that nowhere is there a perfect place or way of life. Wherever you go, there you are.

An American couple, Maureen and Joe, were staying for the winter. Joe had worked for the U.S. Department of State, so he and Maureen had been stationed in many places around the world. He was partially retired, committed to working a certain number of weeks per year. They were trying out Provence as a possible place to settle once Joe no longer worked. They had a sweet little dog, a Lhasa Apso named Dulcinea. We'd often share a cup of coffee or glass of wine, and I would look in on Dulcie if they wanted to be gone for a day. Interacting with them helped me feel at home, but it didn't change a niggling sense that I really wasn't where I was supposed to be. I was searching. Was my old nemesis, Restless, lurking around, ready to pounce?

As the days passed and I had time to reflect, I realized I was going to want to spend even more time in France. It had been a financial stretch to rent the Vue de Ventoux for the winter, but one I had been willing to work with. I'd needed and wanted to come back to the Domaine for one more stay, but looking at the deteriorating condition of the property, I knew it was time to find somewhere else.

November 5, 2005

Mireille came and brought pain au chocolat. She is not happy with Lizzie and Andrew. They are cutting back her work hours and not telling her if she's going to get another contract. Lizzie had the audacity to send me an email asking me to watch for some guests who were due to arrive from Germany and to call Joelle when they got here. Does she forget I'm not working? I'm going to have to tell Joelle this oven needs repairs. Lizzie's going to love hearing that!

AS PART OF MY RENTAL AGREEMENT, I had agreed to feed the cats, which hadn't been a problem in the past. That winter, however, word must have circulated within the cat community: "Ample food at the Domaine des Claparèdes." Cats appeared from nowhere. An all-white male lurked on the garden wall just waiting to pounce on Freddy. One day, I looked up and saw a strange black cat staring in the full-length-glass courtyard door. When I turned around toward the kitchen, I saw another perched on the window ledge. Double vision? I had not been drinking. No, there were two of them. Twins?

After a week of the stray-cat invasion, I went to Apt and bought a live trap. One by one, I trapped the errant felines and transported them down to the valley below the village of Buoux, where there was a hotel catering to rock climbers and horseback riders. I reasoned the cats could easily find shelter in one of the barns on the property. I felt a little guilty, but I knew the SPA, *Société Protectrice des Animaux* (the French equivalent of SPCA), would only euthanize them.

With the cat invasion under control, I would often sit and look out to the courtyard. I was struck by the absolute silence—something I missed in Traverse City. True, there was comfort in the sounds of a city—planes, cars, trains—signs of life, people going about their business, but the sounds could be intrusive. Silence itself seemed to have its own sound, a rhythm, a hum tone, leaving a vacuum to be filled with thoughts. Sometimes I struggled with conflicting thoughts. I loved it here, I truly did. But I also missed Joe, Sally, my condo, and my cats. As I was growing up, I'd often struggled with wanting to be two places at once, and my father used to comment, "You should be twins."

Emotionally and mentally, I struggled. The furnace rattled and made noises in the night. Joelle tried to adjust it, but it was old, and in need of servicing. My surroundings looked shabbier and shabbier. Paint was peeling from shutters; bushes and shrubs were overgrown, and stone walls around the courtyard were crumbling. Then I'd look at the sunny Provençal, blue-winter skies and remember why I'd started coming to the Luberon. The weather was wintry, but it didn't compare to Northern Michigan. The area around Traverse City was known for record snowfall and sub-zero temperatures.

I loved the exercise and camaraderie on the Tuesday walking group Meg organized, and it was via this group I met a Brit couple, Tim and Mary, who were like characters from the old newspaper comic strip, Mutt and Jeff. Tim was a tall, big man with a full head of gray hair, booming voice, and wide, toothy smile. Mary was tiny, with short, dark hair surrounding a round face and twinkling brown eyes. She and I shared an extreme dislike of high places. Often, as we'd be following the group along a narrow, high path, Mary would glance over in my direction and warn, "Don't look down!" Tim and I were among the less speedy walkers, frequently bringing up the rear. We'd often be convulsed with laughter when the path led steeply upwards and we would shout ahead at Meg, "Up!! Up!! Why is it always up?" It wasn't really a criticism of her role as guide but a chance for us to take a break.

One week, as our happy group was strolling along, Mary said, "Jo Anne, don't make any arrangements for next winter. Tim and I want to spend six months touring Australia, and we need someone to come and stay in our house and take care of things." It sounded like a possible solution to my search for housing, and we agreed to keep talking about the option.

FOR THANKSGIVING, Maureen and Joe invited me to celebrate the day with them. Three Americans in Provence; we'd make our own holiday. Maureen prepared an exquisite meal fixing the traditional American fare: roast turkey, stuffing, candied sweet potatoes, and she even found cranberries for sauce.

It felt as if I'd found kindred souls when we shared our feelings about not being attached to place and people. Their years of government assignments in many different locations meant they'd been reluctant to feel too close. You don't want to risk getting emotionally attached to a place when you know you'll soon be obliged to move on. Those thoughts resonated with me as I continued to struggle with feelings of not really belonging anywhere.

November ended with my birthday, but I'd made no plans to celebrate. Mireille came for tea and brought me a plate of her Moroccan spiced cookies and a small cake with a candle. I went to the village post office and picked up a package Joe and Sally had sent containing a very nice photo of Joe and me with his birthday cake. The picture had been taken in September before I left. It was a nice memory … a photo of my brother's birthday for my birthday. I felt the love and warmth and closeness we'd always had before the aborted Christmas trip and after we'd worked through the fall-out from it.

When she left, Mireille had stopped at Maureen and Joe's cottage to tell them it was my birthday. Later, they arrived at my door bearing a fresh raspberry tart. This year was number sixty-nine …. Next year, a big one.

As the day ended, I lit the fire, grabbed my book, and snuggled in, wondering where I'd find myself on my next birthday.

15 Another Venue

MARY AND TIM WERE GOING TO ENGLAND to celebrate the Christmas holiday with family and asked if I'd like to check on the house while they were away and collect their mail. This would allow me time to get a feel for the property. I made several twenty-minute trips from Saignon to their little hamlet near the village of Roussillon. One sunny afternoon, I sat on their terrace enjoying the sun and thought, "This will work. I can be happy here."

When they returned from England, I told them I definitely would take care of their house next winter. The agreement was for me to pay no rent, just utilities, and take care of the mail. It was a perfect solution to my search.

ONE DAY I WAS STROLLING around the Claparèdes property when I heard a gurgling noise. It sounded like a pot of fiercely boiling water. I followed the sound behind one of the cottages and discovered the lid on the septic field was bubbling over! I quickly contacted Joelle, who called Andrew and the plumber. Turns out, the septic tank was plugged. Mireille told me afterwards she'd been talking with the plumber, and apparently Andrew and Lizzie were not paying their bills! The place had become a never-ending stream of problems.

Spring came early to the Luberon, and in March the weather improved, but my morale did not. I got an early-morning message on my mobile phone from a delivery service looking for Andrew. When I called back, the man said Joelle had given him my number. Why mine? No, I did not know where Andrew was. I gave the man Andrew's phone number and hung up. I asked Joelle why the delivery service had my number, and she denied having given it to them.

That evening, at almost 9 p.m., my phone rang once more. This time it was the people renting the Lantins on the other side of Saignon. They wanted to know if this was the weekend we changed to daylight savings time. They said Joelle had given them my number to call if they had questions. I hung up and promptly called Joelle. When she answered, I lost it. I was angry, practically in tears, and ended up yelling. I'd had enough glasses of wine to loosen my tongue, and I let her have it. I was not paying two-hundred-and-fifty euros a week to have people bugging me!

March 12, 2006

The saga continues as a family of Americans arrived in the big house. He came asking me, "Where do they keep the firewood?" And Joelle was not here to meet and greet them and to explain that they'll have to find their own firewood. It is sad.

I LOVED THE CLAPARÈDES, but I felt taken advantage of and wanted to leave. Deep down, I was torn. What about Freddy and Sheba? As I struggled with these conflicting emotions, the frustrations persisted. Between rattling furnaces, malfunctioning stoves, catfights, and shabby surroundings, the Claparèdes was no longer a relaxing place to be.

I put my discontent aside long enough to think about the months ahead. I sent an email to my house sitter, Melissa, proposing she stay on at my Traverse City condo as my housemate for the summer months. It didn't seem fair to expect her to find her own place during peak tourist season, when I'd want her back in September.

Her taking care of the cats, the condo, and mail while I was away had really simplified my life. Gratefully, she agreed to the arrangement.

In spite of the Claparèdes frustrations and Melissa's preparations, I wasn't ready to think about going back to Michigan. I wanted to stay in France longer than my rental contract at the Claparèdes and decided to contact Meg about renting their apartment for a few weeks. She and Stephen were agreeable, and when my contract with Lizzie ended, I went back and stayed in their apartment for two weeks.

I'd come full circle from my first stay in 2004. I spent a relaxing and enjoyable two weeks in the familiar setting with gorgeous views of the vineyards and hills and being around Meg, Stephen, and their sweet dog, Miel.

As I enjoyed the sense of comfort and familiarity, I became concerned about Stephen's health. He was not as strong as I remembered. I knew he'd had some medical concerns, but I wasn't sure exactly what they were.

May 12, 2006

I rode to market with Meg and Stephen. He had to go for blood work at the lab in Apt. He seems frail, and I wonder if they are really getting to the bottom of his problems? Meg and Stephen went to a party in the afternoon, and I took care of Miel. We took a long walk around the vineyard, and then I had her outside with me on the terrace.

I WAS SO CONTENT in the apartment and being able to enjoy the markets and vineyard walks, but inevitably, it was time to leave. Reluctantly, I said good-bye to Meg and Stephen. Mireille and Jean-Claude once again would keep my car and my belongings and, after dropping the suitcases at their house, they took me to the TGV. I was on my way back to Michigan. *Back to Michigan.* I couldn't quite bring myself to say "back home."

Because really, where was home? I didn't know.

16 Home?

IT WORKED WELL having Melissa as a housemate. We divided responsibilities for shopping and meals. The condo had two bedrooms and two bathrooms. My bedroom, bath, and desk area were upstairs in the loft, so I had my space and my privacy. She was gone during the day seeing clients, so we weren't tripping over each other. She also worked part time at a local winery and was often away in the evening and weekends. True, there were times when small annoyances crept in. I was set in my ways and not used to sharing living space. Dirty dishes left in the sink and overflowing wastepaper baskets were not what I was used to. All in all, however, it worked out.

I went to the Traverse City farmer's market, which paled in comparison to the markets in Apt, Lourmarin, and Coustellet. I missed the stalls filled with flowers, the baskets overflowing with juicy tomatoes, peaches, and pears, the vintner offering samples of a local wine, and the African merchant with his woven baskets. I missed the aroma of mint and cilantro wafting from the Moroccan stalls and their vendors calling out their wares in Arabic as well as French.

Over the summer months, old friends drifted in and out, I puttered in my gardens, watched golf on TV, and enjoyed sitting with Beemer and Snowflake. I missed them when I was in France, but I knew that Melissa gave them a lot of TLC.

I often drove to Empire to see Joe and Sally. I loved the peace and quiet of their country home and liked spending time with them. Sometimes it felt difficult to justify my desire to be in France with the distance it put between my family and me. Once again, I heard my father's admonishment: "You should be twins." Some things never change.

When I returned to France, I would be living rent free at Tim and Mary's, but I had expenses: mortgage, condo fees, taxes, and upkeep. I needed to add to my cash flow. Looking around the bedroom, I spied my jewelry box. I no longer needed all of those bracelets, earrings, necklaces, and bobbles. Some of them were gold, and there were ads in the local paper for companies buying gold. I gathered up some pieces, took them in, and walked out one-hundred-and-fifteen dollars to the good.

The sale of the gold had given me a few extra dollars, but it hadn't added much to the plus side of the ledger. Ever aware of my bottom line, I decided to sell my car. I had been storing it for the winter months, saving me the cost of insurance, but with my plan to be at Mary and Tim's over the winter and looking forward to possibly staying in France through the following summer, it made no sense to hang onto the car. I called a long-time contact at a local car dealership and, after some negotiation, he bought my car.

It felt great to have more money in my pocket. I got a rental car for the duration of my Michigan stay and turned my efforts toward departure preparations. I sorted through cupboards and cleared closets. I wanted everything in good shape to turn over to Mélissa.

Before I knew it, September arrived, and I was once again leaving Traverse City.

Au Revoir Michigan…. Bonjour France!

17 Big Birthday

I'D AGREED WITH TIM AND MARY to arrive a week before they departed so I'd have a period of orientation. This one was shorter than the infamous Claparèdes fiasco with Lizzie and Andrew, and a lot more organized. Tim and Mary took off for Australia, leaving me in charge. I was set to enjoy a six-month stay that would prove to be infinitely more relaxing.

September 18, 2006

On the terrace of Mary and Tim's house. Fresh juice, fresh figs, and coffee. And lovely warm sunshine! The weather is gorgeous. Mary and Tim have gone, and the true depth of my adventure begins.

AT MARY AND TIM'S, there were some parallels to my Claparèdes caretaking. Mireille was also Mary's cleaning lady and came every few weeks. Her presence meant long conversations, because she was still a talker, but it kept me updated on my French family. She and her husband, Jean-Claude, helped me haul in firewood, and he replaced a broken light switch (just as he'd done for me at the Claparèdes).

Jean-Claude was tall with dark hair and eyes. His family origins were in the Alsace region of France adjacent to Germany. He'd been in the French Air Force, *L'Armée de L'Aire,* where he'd worked in an office and also drove a bus. He was extremely knowledgeable and competent when it came to household repairs or cars.

November 30, 2006

1936 > 2006 70 years!

It's amazing to think it's the morning of my 70th birthday! There have been many travels along the way. It feels great to have arrived geographically, physically, and emotionally. Looking forward to the day.

I REMEMBERED MY LOW-KEY BIRTHDAY last year at the Claparèdes, when I'd enjoyed coffee with Mireille and raspberry tarte with Maureen and Joe. This year was a big one, and I wanted to celebrate with a party. I bought wine and made hors d'oeuvres. The weather was pleasant, and that evening twenty-six friends filled the living room and kitchen-dining area. And those were just the people who were free that night. It was clear that my circle of friends in France far outnumbered those back in the States. I was delighted, happy, and humbled. I finally felt a real sense of belonging. I almost felt "at home." Almost.

Even after a couple of months, I knew I was not going to be ready to go back to Michigan for the summer. I wanted to find a way to spend the summer in the Luberon. Melissa was taking care of my house and pets. She had assured me that if I could stay on in France through the summer, she could easily manage the condo and the cats. Tim and Mary would return in March; I needed to find somewhere to live.

Knowing Melissa was in place, I called Meg and Stephen and asked if they'd be interested in renting their apartment to me for a year. Would they weigh the cost of their weekly vacation renters, the expense of changeovers, cleaning, etc., give me a good rate, and yet make it work for them financially? We discussed the details and agreed, in March 2007, that I would move into their apartment. I'd come full circle from that summer of 2004.

When Mary and Tim returned from their six months of travel in Australia, I gathered my belongings, prepared to move, and realized just how much stuff I'd accumulated.

Subliminally, perhaps, I was relocating to France.

March 29, 2007

A new locale. It looks chaotic. Boxes all around, but I'll get settled soon. Need patience, as I have no TV or internet yet.

MANY OF THE APARTMENT'S furnishings had come from Meg and Stephen's London house and their country cottage in England, making it a nice mix of the best of what is British with the taste of Provençal. The living area had a sofa and an easy chair, and there was a big old desk in one corner, perfect for my writing.

There was a super fireplace in the apartment. It was the end of March, and although spring came early to the Luberon, the nights were chilly. No one had used the fireplace in years, and I wanted to check it out. I gathered wood, kindling, and newspapers and lit a match. My first attempt proved unsuccessful; the entire apartment filled with smoke. Stephen came down and tried adjusting the height of the grate, but no luck. We tried a variety of cures … put a tile under the grate legs, tipped the grate forward, shoved the grate farther back in the fireplace, all with no success. We could always call the chimney sweep, but then I had a thought.

Mireille and Jean-Claude heated their house from their fireplace, so Jean-Claude was accustomed to cleaning the flue. I made a phone call, and a couple of days later, he came with ladder and tools. He climbed onto the roof, and after several minutes of poking and brushing into the chimney, down came clouds of soot and a hornet's nest. The creatures had taken advantage of the unused flue to establish a nest. No wonder the smoke couldn't escape. Flue now clear, the chimney functioned perfectly well, and I was set to enjoy many an evening in front of the fire.

Before any cozy winter evenings, the upcoming summer beckoned. And just think, this summer I would not be running around taking care of late guests, broken pool gates, or leaking faucets. I could finally, really enjoy a glass of wine on the terrace whenever I wanted without fear of interruption. And, I'd be there to see and smell the lavender in bloom.

So, I was back where I had stayed when I first arrived in 2004. Not only were Meg and Stephen my landlords, they'd become close friends. We often shared a glass of wine or a meal. The hillside position of the house made it easy to connect with them on the upper level, yet we each had our privacy.

Meg and Stephen's dog, Miel, was a lovely pet. Miel, the French word for "honey," was an aptly named blond Labrador. Sweet and well mannered, she'd come from the French equivalent of the Humane Society. She was adorable, but she had a penchant for running away. Leave the door open, and off she'd go. The theory was this behavior was related somehow to her previous owner.

Meg and Stephen had a loyal clientele, and in summer, the apartment next to mine was rented to vacationers. The house did not have a pool, so the guests were often older couples that came to enjoy the views, do some hiking, go to markets, and take advantage of the weather.

One day, I was standing outside the door of my apartment chatting with Stephen and the couple who were vacationing in the apartment next door. Suddenly, there was a whooshing sound and a streak of tan went flying by. "Hey," my neighbor said to Stephen, "wasn't that your dog?" Sure enough. Someone had left the door open.

18 Another Year Chez Meg

May 5, 2007

I'm happy to finally be somewhat settled in the apartment. I've got my desk and dresser, and the TV is working. I paid off one of my credit cards and made big payments on the other two. Gives me more disposable income.

I HAD A LOT OF FLEXIBILITY that year with Meg and Stephen … no responsibilities for renters or pools or house cleaning … except my own. When I gave up my gallery in Glen Arbor, I'd also given up organizing trips for groups of artists. As a spinoff, I'd started my own little business, which I called, "Meet Me in Provence." For a fee, I'd arrange travel and housing for people interested in coming to the area. I could boast behind-the-scenes experience, which would enable them to see things the average tourist would not. I charged a modest fee for everything from picking them up at the TGV train station to booking restaurant meals and taking them to markets. One couple was so apprehensive about driving to the Avignon TGV, they offered to pay me to take them there.

Sometimes I'd arrange housing at the Domaine des Claparèdes, which meant I had to interact with Lizzie, but it allowed me to visit my cat buddies, Sheba and Freddy.

As summer intensified, I thought it would be fun to organize a

July Fourth picnic so Stephen and I could share some American customs with our Brit friends. I purchased ground beef and sausages, which were as close to hot dogs as I could find, and made baked beans and potato salad. The Mistral was blowing that afternoon as we gathered on the terrace, and Stephen manned the grill.

"This burger is done," Stephen announced, "who's ready?"

"I'll take it," replied Wendy. I watched as she carefully assembled the hamburger on its bun and topped it with a bit of mustard and proceeded to attack it delicately with her knife and fork. I didn't dare look at Stephen for fear I'd burst out laughing. "Wendy," I said, "This is an American-style picnic. You pick it up in your hands and bite into it."

Wendy looked up at me briefly, a bit of a puzzled look on her face. "That's okay," she answered, "I tend to be messy." I could tell she was not at all comfortable with the concept. But that wasn't the end of the fun. Stephen and I were amused as her husband proceeded to take the baked beans and spread them on a hot dog bun. Oh well, I thought, I know the Brits love their beans and toast.

In spite of the Mistral and the clash of customs over how to eat picnic fare, I'd enjoyed celebrating Independence Day in France *à l'Américain.* As much as I loved being in France, it was impossible to shake my American roots.

STEPHEN LIKED TO SLEEP IN LATE and was annoyed if Meg reminded him Miel needed her morning walk. Meg confided that she insisted on Stephen walking Miel, because otherwise he would watch TV for hours, play bridge on the computer, and get no exercise. He didn't do any household tasks unless she prodded him. He was happy to sit, oblivious to the jobs needing to be done. I tried to keep a neutral attitude, but it looked to me as if Stephen's behavior was unreasonable and unfair to Meg.

I'd noticed how often he became irritable, even belligerent, over minor issues. I remember one occasion when he'd asked me to look up a book on Amazon.com, and I forgot to do it. He asked me about it the next day, and when I told him I hadn't done it, he grew very angry, stomping away muttering, "Oh, just forget it!" His level of anger was completely disproportionate to the situation. It was puzzling.

I'D MOVED INTO THE APARTMENT in March, directly from my seven months at Tim and Mary's house. I missed Joe and Sally and decided to make a trip to Michigan in August and stay through most of September. The extended visit would allow me to take care of medical appointments and celebrate Joe's birthday with him. It also meant I'd be there to take care of Beemer and Snowy, while Melissa took a trip to Florida to see her grandmother. In addition, even though I wasn't eager to face my finances, I needed to meet with my financial planner and go over my budget.

In late August, I made the journey to Paris on the train and took a next-day flight to Michigan. Melissa picked me up at the airport in Traverse City. There I was … if not where I felt I belonged, at least in the only country where I owned property.

August 30, 2007

Had a meeting with Pete about my finances. He reminded me if I contin-

ued spending at the same rate as I currently am doing, I would be out of money in a matter of a few years. Not what I wanted to hear.

LOGICALLY, I COULD UNDERSTAND that my current life-style was not congruent with my financial resources, but it wasn't as if I were dealing with a finite pot of money, in danger of running dry. I did have my teacher's pension and my Social Security ... a regular income ... well, sort of.

I refused to worry about money for the next few weeks and often visited Joe and Sally, when we'd drive around the countryside, walk the Lake Michigan beaches, and enjoy cooking out. Joe had always been a great cook, and his bar-b-que ribs, slow-cooked on the grill, were the kind to set you drooling at the mere mention of them.

I had a superb visit and felt sad at the prospect of leaving people and pets behind, but when the autumnal equinox arrived, I said final goodbyes and left for France. The changing seasons felt like the appropriate time for changes in my life.

19 Back To The Luberon

SEPTEMBER AND OCTOBER WEATHER in Provence was wonderfully mild. It felt good to be with my customary morning views of the hills and the vineyards. Ah … *la vie en rose* and excellent *rosé*. I lapsed into my customary junkets to market and walking around the vineyard with Miel. I felt my entire being unwind. Physically and mentally, I relaxed.

November arrived, and out of deference to Stephen (and a little to me, too, I think), Meg prepared a luscious Thanksgiving meal inviting a few Brit friends to join us. Another Thanksgiving in France. Last year, I'd been taking care of Mary and Tim's house while they were in Australia. Meg had gone to England to visit her sister, and I'd made a Thanksgiving meal for Stephen and Elizabeth. The previous year, there'd been Thanksgiving at the Claparèdes with Maureen and Joe. We Americans did our best to make our customs and holidays fit into our life in France. Once again, there was that reminder that I was living with one foot in two different cultures, and at times it felt like I was doing the splits to keep my equilibrium.

Right after Thanksgiving, Meg went to England to visit her sister, and Stephen stayed home with Miel. I would sometimes take her for a walk to give him a break. He often complained of a bad back, though I was never sure how bad it was, or if he was just tired of walking the dog. Stephen was an enigma. He could be short and

curt and distant. And then later the same day, he'd be chatty and friendly. I wondered about his health. He was agreeable enough most of the time, but I felt sorry for him. I thought he wasn't very happy, or maybe had some medical issues.

With Meg in England, Stephen invited me for supper to celebrate my birthday. I confess I had my trepidations, but I accepted. After all, it was just upstairs. To my delight, he had chilled a bottle of champagne and fixed a delicious fettuccini Alfredo.

While I was there, Meg called from England to wish me a happy birthday. She had a miserable cold and sounded dreadful. I'd never spent any time in England, but it seemed to me every time one of my Brit friends went over to visit, they came back with a nasty head cold. Must be why they'd opted to live in Provence. I couldn't fault them for it. I'd left Northern Michigan for similar reasons.

20 New Venture – New Venue

CHRISTMAS HOLIDAYS WERE APPROACHING, but I didn't have a lot of preparation to do, because I'd be spending the holiday taking care of a house and cats in the village of Roussillon on the other side of Apt. Early in September, I'd gotten a call from a friend of Meg's asking if I'd be interested in doing some house- and cat-sitting over the Christmas holiday. She'd put me in touch with a Brit couple that had a house just below Roussillon. I drove over to meet Paul and Anne and their cats.

Anne was medium height and stature, had short, light-brown hair that was streaked blond, and friendly, blue eyes. She had an infectious laugh, a quick wit, and her lilting voice retained its British accent. She also had a no-nonsense manner about her, which I was sure worked well in organizing the trips for clients of the "Real Provence" tour business they ran out of their home office. They took care of a number of rental houses in the area, including one they owned, and set up tours for people wanting to come for a visit.

Paul was fairly tall. His balding head no longer bore evidence of the curly mop of dark hair shown in his Facebook photo, but his brown eyes and mischievous smile were the same. He did some watercolor painting, an activity that seemed to me a stark contrast to his IT training. That technical side was put to good use as he designed and monitored the websites for their business.

They'd moved to France fifteen years earlier and now had three cats. We talked, and I agreed to come stay for the holiday. It would allow them to visit family in England and add euros to my bank account.

Pre-holiday December, Apt was again festooned in brilliant Christmas lights. I remember the first Christmas I saw those lights made by the Blachère Company. They might have been the Paris hand-me-downs from the previous year, but they looked extraordinary.

December 19, 2007

Settled in here at Paul and Anne's house. I'm warm and cozy … gorgeous views, a nice comfy bed AND fabulous high-speed internet. The cats are sweet, especially Sebastian, a white male they call Sebby. He pawed around the bed last night. The other two, Frankie and Ellie, both females, are a bit more distant. (I asked about Frankie's name. Seems when they got her as a kitten they thought she was a male, and the name stuck.) She's a tabby and looks a lot like Sheba and Freddy. Ellie has long beige fur with black legs and paws.

CHRISTMAS DAY. I'd been invited to join several ex-pat couples, including Meg and Stephen, at the home of a Brit couple. We were treated to homemade cream soup, roasted ham, vegetables, the customary cheese board, and a lot of wine. After a pause ... dessert. Mindful of approaching darkness and hungry cats, I left after dessert and made the drive back to Roussillon.

December 26, 2007

Last evening, I found myself champing at the bit to leave. We did sing carols, which was O.K., but it went on a bit. Maybe I'm resisting being sucked into a pattern of socialization where I feel I don't fit. I sense quite a class and cultural difference in how I've lived compared to the Brits and South Africans.

I ENDED MY HOLIDAY STAY with Paul and Anne's cats and, a few days after Christmas, I made the trek back to my apartment in Saignon. I politely declined invitations and spent a quiet New Year's Eve on my own. It had been years since I'd gotten excited about balloons, confetti, and noisemakers.

In mid-January, an American family, clients of my "Meet Me in Provence" business, arrived. I had put them in touch with Lizzie, and they'd arranged to stay in one of the cottages at the Claparèdes.

January 5, 2008

I went to the Claparèdes yesterday. I took some firewood for the American couple and talked to Joelle for an hour. She is really discouraged. The cottages are looking shabby. One of the shutters on the door to the Borie is hanging half off. I saw Freddy, and he looked good, but he followed me out to the road and looked pitiful sitting there as I drove away.

AS THE WINTER PROGRESSED, I had a visit from my old friend Restless. Wow! It had been quite a while since he (or was it she?) came calling. I'm not sure what prompted it. Had I unwittingly issued an invitation? The weather was uncharacteristically gray and rainy. Was that the trigger? Where was the Provençal blue sky?

I was loath to admit I didn't enjoy my apartment as much in the winter months. The view was fantastic, but it was dark. I hadn't realized just how much being built into the hillside, all windows north-facing, would restrict any amount of sunlight, or even regular light, during the shorter winter days.

I'd told Joelle I would go up to the Claparèdes from time to time to check on the cats and be sure they had food. It would give me a chance to see Freddy and to enjoy some sunshine.

January 22, 2008

Went up to the Claparèdes yesterday around 3 P.M. The cats were all sitting and waiting. Hungry! I fed them, gathered some wood. I've offered to feed the cats three days this week and next.

January 30, 2008

Yesterday, the Claparèdes fiasco continued. I got a call from the laundry service that the gates would not open. (It seems they still have MY phone number.) I went up later to flip the fuse and feed the cats. It seems that Andrew (?) has taken all of the keys. I called Joelle. She's off on a trip with school children ... and was livid. She was cursing and saying she was going to quit. S.S.D.D. I fed the cats and left. Gratefully, there's a family coming in on Saturday, and they can feed the cats.

THE VISITS TO THE CLAPARÈDES and the phone calls brought back memories of my time there as guardian. In retrospect, I felt good about how well I'd survived, but wondered how I could have been naive enough to think it would be a walk in the park. The hassles of the upkeep and the conflicts with Lizzie were not memories I wanted to cherish. It was hard to believe it had been a few years ago. My time in France always seemed to go faster than I wanted it to.

Warmer weather in March encouraged the daffodils and forsythia to blossom. This was more like it ... Provençal blue skies, mild temperatures, and sunshine. But spring also meant thinking about a change of housing.

I hadn't decided on next winter's venue, but I did have choices. I'd hedged with Meg and Stephen about their apartment. Sometimes it's a case of better the devil you know, but I had to be honest with myself about the lack of high speed internet, and in the dead of winter, the lack of light. Even with the indecision, I had to face reality, and, reluctantly, I started packing.

Then, shortly before my scheduled departure in mid-March, Anne phoned.

"Jo Anne," she said, "Paul and I have been talking, and we have an idea." She explained Paul had a contract with a small company and would be in London much of the time.

"We both love London, and Paul has a small flat there. Instead of Paul coming back to France periodically, I'd like to go join him." She proposed I live in one of their rental houses next winter and, in lieu of payment, stay with their cats whenever she joined Paul in London.

"We also plan to be in England over Christmas to visit family," she added. "Plus, we're toying with a winter vacation in South Africa." It sounded perfect, and I accepted with glee. At last, I knew where I would be next winter! And "free" was *well* within my budget.

I thought about my pattern of looking for where I'd live since my first visit in 2003 and my tour of duty as a guardian in 2004. I was probably predestined to do the Claparèdes repeat in the winter of 2005-2006, but from that point on it had been a cycle of search, find, settle on, and then repeat the following year. Nothing ever fell into place long term. I was tied to Michigan and to my Traverse City condo. I had created this ping-pong existence of living on two continents, which was okay, but didn't exactly lend itself to feelings of stability.

The year in my apartment at Meg and Stephen's had streaked by faster than Miel on a getaway. In March 2008, I said *au revoir* to my Luberon friends and went back to Michigan for the summer.

21 Mich- again

Traverse City, March 15, 2008

....And so, one phase ends and another begins. I'm back in Michigan with mixed feelings. I called Joe and Sally. Melissa arrived from her office around 7:30 PM, and we had a soup-and-salad supper.

SOON AFTER I ARRIVED BACK, Melissa left for a trip to Australia. The timing was perfect as it gave me a chance to re-enter my life in the States while having the condo entirely to myself. We'd gotten along really well in the past, but I was so used to doing things my own way, I sometimes had expectations not in alignment with her behavior. Not her fault, not mine either, it just was what it was.

I had a rough time getting adjusted to northern Michigan weather, time change, and life in the States. I had been looking forward to being in Traverse City for the summer. The weather would be great, I'd be near Joe and Sally, I could settle into my condo with Beemer and Snowy, and see friends. Once there, however, it didn't take long for me to start missing my Luberon life: the walks around the vineyard, the merchants hawking their wares at markets, coffee in the café, and even my exercise classes at the gym I'd joined. Nothing felt right. I had a rotten case of amplified and extended jet lag.

What struck me was how accustomed I'd become to quieter surroundings, a slower pace, and the ease of life in Provence. Suddenly, everything was noisy and supersized! Sirens blew day and night, and planes landing at the nearby airport often felt as if they were grazing my roof. I'd pull up to the traffic light in my mid-sized rental car only to realize I was dwarfed on both sides by humungous SUVs. I felt like the filling in an SUV sandwich.

Restaurants served big portions. You took it with you in a doggy bag. What if you didn't have a doggy? No matter. You got lots of whatever it was you ordered whether or not you were able to eat all of it. Out in public, everyone spoke with loud voices. The din was incessant, and I felt completely out of sync.

One day in particular, the contrast really hit me. It was at a grocery store (in France we say "supermarket"), a big-box store, and I was doing my weekly shopping. In France, shoppers are always greeted with "Bonjour," and it didn't matter if you approached a clerk at the hardware store seeking information, or if you were putting your groceries on the belt in the checkout, you always exchanged a "Bonjour."

I'd gotten my groceries unloaded from the cart and had a moment's hiccup when I remembered, unlike in France, I would not be bagging them myself. Bags all loaded into my cart, I'd turned for the clerk's usual, "*Au Revoir. Bonne journée.*" Forget good-bye and have a nice day in America, she was already on to the next person in line. She wasn't being purposefully rude, but I was no longer in her consciousness. For me, now well accustomed to the lovely French manners, even in everyday situations, it was jarring.

I'd sold my car before leaving for my year in France, had rented one when I arrived back in Traverse City, but now I needed to buy a car. I started looking online and at the ads in the paper. I didn't enjoy the process, as it involved spending a considerable sum of money. I had to find a suitable vehicle. Suitable to drive, and to pay for.

I had car woes, plus it was nearing income tax time. I needed to prepare papers for the CPA. Damned money issues would not go away. It didn't matter that I was officially a senior citizen; I had a powerful urge to throw myself on the floor and have a good old-fashioned temper tantrum.

Deciding to face the car issue, I called a salesman who had been helpful to me over the years. "There are several good used cars on the lot, Jo Anne," he said, "Come on over this afternoon and drive a couple."

In the afternoon I went over to the dealership, did a few test drives, and bought a used Toyota. It was a five-year-old, mid-sized vehicle that had come up from Florida, which meant it had not been subjected to the rigors of Michigan winter's road salt. The mileage was low and the price was right! Only after it was mine, parked under the carport at my condo, did I begin to think of my car adventures both in France and the U.S. I was now the proud owner of two cars, both Toyotas, and both almost the same gun-metal gray. And the Michigan version was small. Had my French persona followed me here?

In Traverse City, hordes of summer tourists flocked into town, reminding me of summers in Apt. But unlike France, it wasn't a leisurely vacation. Here it was hurry, hurry, hurry. Didn't anyone ever slow down? Multi-tasking was a way of life for Americans. Look at the map while driving the car while licking an ice cream cone. Hurry, hurry, never mind the speed limit, we are in a hurry to get to the beach.

Oh, how I hated it! I sure couldn't imagine these people relaxing over a cup of coffee for a couple of hours in a café, or strolling the cobblestone streets in Apt.

In addition to the hassles of navigating life amidst tourists, I experienced hassles with fellow owners in our condominium. When Rod and I had first started living in the complex, we were a pretty cohesive group of first-time owners. As the years went on, some of those original owners moved out, and things became noticeably less pleasant.

A single mom with a young son bought one unit. The houses and the property were not intended to have children in residence, but there were no restrictions against it. When Rod and I had mentioned the possibility to the builder, he brushed it off. "No one with kids is going to want to live here," he'd said. "We're on a busy main thoroughfare, and there really is no yard for kids to play in." *Au contraire mon frère.* The gardens I painstakingly groomed around my condo often suffered as the boy and his pals chased down an errant ball and played tag in the courtyard.

Melissa returned from her trip to Australia. Gradually we settled in to our house-sharing arrangement. At times I missed being on my own, but I greatly appreciated the help with household expenses, and I was comforted knowing she'd care for the condo and the cats when I went back to France in the fall.

> *May 10, 2008*
>
> *Went to Joe and Sally's the day before yesterday. Sally is going on a trip with the school and Joe asked if I'd come out and visit and help with the dog. There was no doggy day care where they usually take Will. I spent the day, night, and most of yesterday. We hiked the Empire Bluff trail, and it was gorgeous. It's so peaceful out there. It makes me realize that I really prefer the country. I'm having trouble feeling oriented and happy here.*

JOE AND SALLY had acquired their dog, Will, shortly after their first dog, Maggie, went skipping off to doggy heaven. A Cairn Terrier, just like Toto in the Wizard of Oz, Will was a handful. He was all terrier and no matter how many dog obedience classes he aced, he continued to chew up his soft toys and if they let him off the leash, he'd run away. Sally adored him. Joe tolerated him.

Late August I got an email from Anne saying Paul's job had changed, and he was not going to keep his flat in London, so she wouldn't be going over to be with him. However, she reiterated the offer of their free rental house, because they would be doing some traveling. She asked if I could come stay with the cats over the Christmas holiday, and I was hugely relieved.

22 Down and Up

SAYING GOODBYE TO JOE, SALLY, WILL, MELISSA, and the cats was not easy. I continued to feel quite torn between the anticipation of getting back to France and the sadness at saying goodbye to my family, friends, and pets, but travel day came and I was off, over the great ocean.

What had once felt like such a daunting journey was now a familiar trek. To the airport, a connection in Detroit, over the ocean, and then landing in Paris. Clear immigration. Clear customs. Pick up my suitcases, head to the train and on to Avignon.

Once there, dear Jean-Claude and Mireille were waiting for me, and got me to Paul and Anne's rental house tucked in the trees. I was eager to get established into a new venue and resume my familiar activities. I had a widening circle of friends, both ex-pats and French. My life was less and less in Michigan, and more and more in my adopted country. I felt amazingly comfortable in my new digs. In December, Paul and Anne left for England, and I went to their house for what would become my annual Christmas cat care.

CHRISTMAS DAY WAS OVER and I relaxed. Sunday evening, I prepared the cats' supper. The three were quite different in temperament as well as the degree to which they would grace me with their presence. Sebastian, AKA "Sebby," was all white and always around.

Sebby loved to eat, and his girth reflected this pleasure. He wasn't fat. He was stout. Each night he'd join me to claim his share of the bed and pillows. I'd never been able to figure out how a small animal can be such a big presence. I'd often wake in the morning, hunched at the edge of the bed, with Sebby pressed against my back.

But that Sunday evening, he was noticeably absent at dinnertime. "Odd," I thought. I put food out for the other two and went upstairs to see if I could rouse Sebby by calling out my bedroom window. As I was about to call his name, I glanced down at a chair in the corner. There he was, just lying there. A quick examination revealed he clearly was not well. I coaxed him a bit, and he ventured down the stairs. Just as he scurried to hide under the table, I noticed he was limping.

It was a Sunday, and evening on top of it! I quickly found the phone number for the vet's office, all the while praying there'd at least be one vet, somewhere in the area, on emergency call. I was amazed when a vet answered. After a brief conversation, she offered to see the cat, but I'd have to bring him in immediately.

The vet's office was a good twenty-minute drive, and it was already dark! I did not like driving after dark, and I'd planned to fill the almost empty gas tank the next morning. I grabbed the travel carrier (always ready, just in case), quickly wrapped Sebby in a towel, and thrust him into it. Clearly, if he was not well, he was doing a masterful job of hiding it. He repeatedly flung himself against the sides of the carrier, yowling loudly. I made the drive with Sebby howling and banging, my eyes glued to the gas gauge.

Once inside the vet's office, it became obvious the only way Sebby was going to submit to being examined was if he were completely sedated. It took both the vet and her assistant to administer the sedative.

The vet and I watched as the shot took effect, and then she began to poke and prod. Finally, she found the damage. Sebby had been attacked by something and had two deep and nasty bites on his foreleg. I say "attacked," because Sebby would never pick a fight. I knew he'd go out of his way to avoid confrontation, even with his housemates. The vet administered a shot for pain and a shot of antibiotic.

Once assured he was waking up, we placed him gently in the carrier, and I made the trip back, with a much more subdued Sebastian.

My feline friend survived the episode, but for several days he did not venture far afield. I was grateful and relieved I'd been able to get him quickly cared for on a Sunday evening. I also forgave him his regular attempts to take my share of the bed and resolved to keep more gas in the car at all times, just in case!

During the winter, I spent weeks with Sebby, Ellie, and Frankie, while their owners did more traveling. It wasn't long, however, before I started to think ahead to the next year.

This housing arrangement was temporary. I knew I wanted to stay in France again, but *where?*

I was mucking around in my head over this housing conundrum when I got a call from an American woman, "Sally" (not my sister-in-law Sally, but Sally from Saignon). I'd become acquainted with Sally in 2004, when I was taking care of Lizzie and Andrew's properties. Lizzie had given me Sally's name and that of her French husband, Marcel, as people I could contact should I need assistance. They lived just below the village, not too far from Meg and Stephen.

Marcel and Sally had moved permanently from California to France a number of years ago. It was while they were living in California that they'd become good friends with a couple, Gary and Cathy. A few years ago, Gary and Cathy had come to France for an extended visit. According to the story, Gary and Cathy were walking around Saignon the day before they were to go back to the States, saw a "for sale" sign on a property in the village, and the rest, as the saying goes, was history.

Now, Gary and Cathy were looking for someone to stay in the Saignon house next winter, when they'd be back in New York. Aware of my previous experience as a guardian, Sally suggested my name to Gary. With Gary's approval, she'd arranged for me to visit the Saignon property.

"I'VE OPENED ALL OF THE SHUTTERS," Sally said, "so you can see there's a lot of sunshine, even this time of year." It was, in fact, early springtime 2009, and I was looking at a potential rental for the following winter in the center of Saignon.

"You know how we Americans are!!" Sally said. "We need lots of sunshine and have to be warm."

"Why do you think I've opted not to spend any more winters in Northern Michigan?" I replied.

We were in the house, which had been three separate village residences, one in partial ruin. Village houses are traditionally narrow and built on three or four levels. Like all of the houses on this edge of Saignon, its outer walls had been part of the ancient ramparts where, ages ago, sentinels walked guard duty. Here it was again. This sense of history … permanence.

Under the house was what could best be called a basement, a cave (the French pronounce it "cahhhvh"), a base of the ancient ramparts which had once extended underground all around the village before owners had built walls between properties. It was like a scary old cellar … stone steps down, stone walls around, and stone ceiling overhead. It was, quite literally, a cave.

Once they purchased the Saignon property, Gary and Cathy hired an architect and began restoration and renovation. The three narrow buildings became one large house under the architectural guidance of none other than Andrew—of the Claparèdes Lizzie and Andrew!

Gary and Cathy had a small apartment in New York City, which served as a base for Cathy, whose work in public relations necessitated her being near corporate offices much of the year. Gary had authored books on British Naval History and bought and sold collectible books, which meant he could work anywhere. The year after the Saignon property was completed, Gary began spending his summers there, but he wasn't around after November. The first winter after their restoration had been mostly completed, they'd left the house empty, and there'd been a huge problem with mold and mildew on the walls. They wanted the house warm, lived in, and final details of restoration completed.

The living-dining area was bright with sunshine beaming through the windows. We climbed to the bedroom level via a spiral staircase, which Andrew had designed to be aesthetically and architecturally pleasing, but it was completely open to the three floors below. Lovely to look at but a tad scary when climbing or descending! Fortunately, there was an artisanal wrought-iron railing against the wall. I made a mental note, "don't look down!"

"Here's the guest bedroom and bath. This would be yours." Sally gestured toward a large, sun-filled bedroom, with a view over Saignon's rooftops, the valley and the town of Apt. Almond blossoms bathed the hillsides in a beautiful pink hue. I looked around, gazed at the almond blossoms, and knew it could very well be where I'd spend next winter.

And so, I began email negotiations with a couple I'd never met. Ultimately, we agreed on a rental price, and with an email handshake, I was set. Later that year, in November 2009 (exact date not yet determined), I would begin what evolved into a five-year period of winter stays on the rue Cilly in the heart of Saignon.

Gary arrived for his summer stay a couple of weeks before I was due to leave for Michigan. Since he wouldn't be there in November when I came back, we agreed it would be a good idea for him to show me a few things about the house.

"WATCH YOUR HEAD," Gary directed, as we descended the stone steps leading down to the cave. I ducked to clear the arched opening above the stairs, and gingerly made my descent.

Somewhere in his fifties, Gary had a stocky, medium build, dimpled cheeks, and a quick laugh. He was slightly balding and wore dark-rimmed glasses. Years of living in the States had not erased his British accent.

We made our way through a dusty, narrow walkway under yet another arched entry. I remembered this cave had originally extended under three separate houses. "I'll show you where the box is for the heating system." Gary proudly pointed to a box on the wall. "There are two windows on the box. This one indicates the temperature of the water, and the other shows water pressure."

I was about to get my indoctrination into Gary's House Heating 101. I took a small measure of confidence from all my experience with the houses and electrical systems at the Claparèdes. I would

later discover this heating system was an animal of a different era, but for the moment I was okay with his instructions. Gary explained he'd hired a local man, Alain, who'd keep an eye on things and help me out if needed. The visit over, I shook hands with Gary and went back to my house. I relaxed; my annual search for next year's housing was done.

Departure day, I drove to Mireille and Jean-Claude's house, where we unloaded my suitcases and boxes from the car. I was fortunate they were willing and had the space to keep things safe and dry in the garage under their house and my car in the yard. "*On y va!*" And with a "Let's go!" we hopped into Mireille's car to the TGV station in Avignon. I began the now familiar trek ... a return to Michigan.

DURING THE WINTER, Melissa had purchased a house and was finalizing her move. I no longer had a built-in house sitter, nor did I have a housemate. Happily for me (and for them), she had agreed to take Beemer and Snowy to her new place when I went to France in the fall. I knew how lucky I was to have such a convenient arrangement. Even during the summer, if I wanted to be gone for a few days, Melissa would keep the cats.

June 18, 2009

I worked on my gardens for an hour yesterday. I keep having nigglings that I want to sell. I want to move on ... maybe go to France for 6 or 8 months ... or a year. Sigh. What to do.

I GOT EMAILS FROM GARY AND CATHY about their Saignon house, and we finalized an exact move-in date. The rent was reasonable, and I could pay in dollars, not euros. This was a real coup, because it meant I would know exactly how much money I was spending on rent each month. If I paid in euros, the price would be subject to the whims of the exchange rate, and that rate never seemed to be in favor of the dollar.

Since Melissa had moved, I decided not to have a house sitter. I hired a handyman to do some painting, and he would check in on the condo while I was away.

September 14, 2009

Went to Joe and Sally's for a belated birthday celebration for Joe and took along a carrot cake with a candle. Joe grilled chicken on the Weber and we took a short walk through the woods.

I ENJOYED MY FIRST CRISPY, crunchy Michigan apple of the season as I anticipated the first frost. I did not want to be in Michigan!! I wanted to be in France, and yet I had the familiar mixed feelings about my departure. I was impatient to see my Provençal friends (both human and animal). I wanted to walk the streets of Apt and go to the markets. I wanted to grab a fresh baguette from *Chez Christine's* little bakery in Saignon. On the other hand, it had been a summer of quality time with Joe and Sally, and it was going to be hard leaving them, and Will, as wild as he was. I was going to miss the furry little guy AND my cats!

November 28, 2009

I had a really nice Thanksgiving and couple of days with Joe and Sally. Turkey dinner was great. Seems good to celebrate Thanksgiving in the States with my real family.

A COUPLE OF DAYS PRIOR TO MY FLIGHT to Paris, I took Beemer and Snowy over to Melissa's house. Having stayed there periodically over the summer, they were right at home. As soon as they were out of the carrying kennels, they sniffed around the living room and went off to stare out the window at the birds and squirrels. I could leave for France without feeling as if I were abandoning my pets.

A new experience was waiting for me. I was a little apprehensive, but I remembered my first year at the Claparèdes. I'd marched into the unknown and, excepting my troubles with Lizzie, it had turned out just fine.

23 Where it all began

December 3, 2009 Rue Cilly – The Village of Saignon

It's pouring rain, but a glorious feeling to be here. A charming man on the TGV platform picked up my suitcases without asking and helped me onto the train and off in Avignon. Mireille and Jean-Claude were there. We stopped by their house to pick up my things and provisions, which Mireille had purchased. Gary's guardien, Alain, met us and showed us around.

I WAS BACK IN SAIGNON, where it all began for me. Sometimes it felt as if I'd time traveled. Saignon, "my" village. Maybe I lived here in another life, it felt so familiar. I remembered that first summer, 2004, when Lizzie had arranged for me to stay in the studio apartment for one week. Now I was just down the lane and in an enormous house.

Saignon was a travelogue picture of medieval stone houses and narrow, winding, cobblestone streets. Perched high above the surrounding area, it had been built this way so an approaching enemy would never surprise its residents. I was living with history; these walls had survived for centuries.

The population was just over 1,000, give or take a few. There was an elementary school, a small hotel, Christine's bakery, several restaurants (mostly seasonal), and a main square with a bubbling fountain.

I'd always thought I didn't want to live in the village, because I needed to be able to step outside and enjoy a cup of coffee or an evening glass of wine with only the scenery to keep me company. Village houses don't have porches. The doors open directly onto the street. Gary and Cathy's house, however, had a very large terrace on the second floor, just off the kitchen, with fabulous views of the surrounding area and the town of Apt below in the valley.

I spent a couple of weeks getting oriented to the house and getting in touch with Meg and others. I did a refresher on Gary's earlier introduction to the house's heating system and what it required. Then, on December 21, I headed to Roussillon for my third year's Christmas stay with Paul and Anne's cats.

December 23, 2009

Chez Paul & Anne in Roussillon

I just saw a gorgeous daybreak with clouds and mist over the valley and the pink sky above the hills of the Luberon. I am SO enjoying being here.

I'D BEEN INVITED TO MIREILLE and Jean-Claude's house for Christmas Day. I arrived at 11:30 a.m. for *apéritif.* Thirteen of us gathered enjoying rum-based fruit punch and a traditional holiday-stuffed bread appetizer, which was a tall round loaf of dark bread horizontally sliced and layered with ham, salmon, and cheese, then reassembled and cut into vertical wedges. A super sandwich! Sisters, brothers, cousins, and in-laws all sipped and munched. It tested my ability with the language to follow the rapid conversation and keep track of which cousin belonged to which brother.

The French eat a *lot* of seafood at Christmastime, and, after *apéritif,* Mireille's brother shucked oysters from a large box on the kitchen counter. When the oyster plates were ready, the call came: *"A table!"* "Let's eat!"

Wine was poured and toasts offered. Oysters flanked by lemon wedges were accompanied by small rounds of thinly sliced sweet bread and salted butter. Most butter served in France is of the unsalted variety, but oysters called for the salted kind.

Next came a course of chilled green beans, thinly sliced fresh mushrooms, and a slice of *foie gras,* all sprinkled with walnuts and freshly made vinaigrette. The main dish was pork roasted in vermouth and mushrooms served with fresh tagliatelle in a white-wine crème-fraîche sauce, sprinkled with grated emmenthal cheese. Clearly, calories and cholesterol were not being considered in this feast.

No meal in France is complete without the cheese platter, which was followed by a lettuce salad. I'd always loved the French tradition of serving salad after the main course, which is supposed to help digestion. My digestion needed it!

There was an appropriate pause to clear the dishes and re-organize the table, then dessert. Mireille had made two of the traditional Yule log cakes, *Bûche de Noël.* I thought back to the Christmas at the Claparèdes, when Mireille had first introduced me to these Christmas cakes. Each resembled a log, frosted with rich chocolaty icing, and decorated with tiny figures of trees, men with saws in hand, and deer. The exterior was an artistic creation. The interior ... a recipe for clogged arteries. A thin layer of rich, yellow cake had been topped with layers of butter and cream then rolled, jellyroll fashion, into the log. I thought of my medical tests in Michigan. My cholesterol count had been perfect, but I persuaded Mireille to cut my slice paper-thin.

Finally, out came the traditional Provençal thirteen desserts. These consisted of dried fruits, nougat, and nuts. We nibbled on a few of the items … more for the keeping of tradition than for sating of appetites for sweets.

There was a post-dinner cup of coffee, and at 4 p.m., I made my exit. Back in Roussillon with Paul and Anne's cats, I wrapped myself in a warm feeling of contentment. I had spent Christmas day with my French family.

December 31, 2009

It's gray and heavy cloud cover. Yesterday turned gorgeous. 64 degrees! This is the third New Year's Eve I've spent here with the cats, just perfect.

I'D RETURNED FROM CAT SITTING in Roussillon and, for the third day, I was sitting snowbound in Saignon. I could hear my own voice smugly stating, "Oh, it may snow in the Luberon a couple of times during the winter, but never more than an inch or two at most. And, it melts almost immediately." *Au contraire ma soeur!* I was happy I'd gotten back after my holiday cat-sitting gig in Roussillon. There would be no moving now.

January 10, 2010

After rain yesterday, snow!! It's a slushy, frozen mess. Looks like I won't be going anywhere for a few more days. Maybe I'll walk up to Christine's bakery today.

THE WARNINGS HAD BEGUN EARLY in the week, and by Thursday night, it was coming down. I was going nowhere. My car was parked on the quay, the narrow, one-way street below the house; at least I thought my car was down there under that mound of snow. Last winter's weather had been unusual, but this one was starting out even crazier.

I watched what passed for the village snowplow—a small tractor—more like a riding lawnmower—with a blade pulled behind, driven by Christine's husband. In addition to helping her at *Chez Christine* bakery, he worked for the village. He made a pass down our narrow lane, then circled around and came back up the quay to the village. The road followed the old ramparts, which were part of the original village walls. I thought about the walls of the house where I was comfortably sitting, all warm and cozy. I felt pretty darn secure. These walls had been part of the ancient ramparts, and no snowstorm was going to affect them.

By Saturday, I was actually having a pretty good time. Forced detention meant time to read books and listen to the radio (no TV yet installed). Night was settling in, I had the fireplace and candles glowing—and then, POOFFFF, off went the electricity.

All day the radio had been announcing the possibility of rolling blackouts. I glanced around … streetlights: on … lights in the neighbor's house: on. This was not a good sign. If all others had electricity, the problem clearly was mine. I grabbed a flashlight and went down to the garage and the fuse box … the main switch: off. I tried repeatedly to reset it, but without success.

I called Alain, who lived on the other side of the village. He said there was no way he could use his car, but he'd get bundled up and walk over. He arrived about twenty minutes later. Shedding his heavy parka, he stomped the snow from his boots. We spent almost half an hour going up and down, back and forth, into the scary basement cave. He finally located a switch in a fuse box, which controlled the hot water heater and furnace, as well as a few lights in the cave. One of them was the culprit. Water had gotten into the lines, but thanks to him, the electricity was back on.

"*Du vin?*" I asked, offering him a glass of wine.

"*Oui, merci,*" he agreed, and I poured us both a glass of local red.

Offering a glass of wine was the least I could do. As we did a quick assessment of my housebound situation, he questioned, "*Vous-avez du pain?*"

Ah, did I have bread?

Bread, the staff of life and the heart of everything French. I'd learned that for the French, everything revolved around "our daily bread."

"*Oui, bien sûr,*" I assured him.

I had bread and even two baguettes in the freezer. Reassured, Alain bundled up, grabbed his flashlight and trudged off into the dark and cold. I watched as the figure and flashlight disappeared into the wall of snow. From Sunday night veterinary services to Saturday evening household guardians, French angels came in many forms.

THE COUPLE WHO LIVED JUST ACROSS the lane, Regis and Nadette, were natives of Saignon. Earlier in the week I'd been attempting to clear the snow from my car and Regis had appeared outside. He was short and stocky with a tanned, craggy face and gnarled hands—mute evidence of hours spent tending grapevines in all kinds of weather. I introduced myself to him and later to Nadette, who had short, brown hair and a beaming smile, dressed casually in slacks and a light jacket.

One never knew how the natives would accept a foreigner (and an American to boot). I must have passed some invisible test, because they offered to loan me a shovel. I gratefully accepted, knowing there was no other way to dig out. Gary had a lot of tools and equipment, but a snow shovel was not among the collection. I'm sure he didn't expect I'd need one.

The next day I was finishing up my digging when Nadette introduced me to her sister-in-law, who lived just down the lane. A chatty grandmother, Mireille (did being chatty and being named Mireille go together?) was equally warm and friendly.

I was extremely pleased when Nadette asked me to join the three of them for afternoon tea. It was a good feeling to sit with French people—well-known natives of the village. To be accepted by ex-pats was one thing, but to be welcomed by villagers was special.

Living in the heart of the village was new to me, but I liked it.

The neighbors waved and called out *"Bonjour, Jo Anne."* (In France, it is customary to include the person's name when you are greeting them.) My French was pretty good, and I think it made a difference as to how quickly I was accepted as a "villager."

My first winter on the rue Cilly was enjoyable, albeit with a high learning curve. With the house itself, I had my work cut out for me. I thought I knew a lot about property care when I was *guardienne* at the Claparèdes. But Gary and Cathy's house was a home, not a rental property. There were finishing touches to the restoration needing to be done, and, at Gary's request, I'd contacted various artisans arranging for iron curtain rods to be made and installed, as well as for repair of the gorgeous, heavy, oak door leading onto the street. I hoped Gary would be pleased when he got here to see the improvements first hand.

SHORTLY AFTER MY ARRIVAL, I'd joined a gym in Apt called Megaform (I loved that name.) I started going to exercise classes and enjoyed interacting with the (mostly) French participants. It was where I met Brigitte and Nicole, a couple who lived in the village of Goult, on the other side of Apt from Saignon.

Brigitte was short and bisexual. Her gray hair was cut man-style short, and she sported tattoos on her neck and arm. An excellent self-taught artist, she'd been born in France but left to live first in Canada and then on the East Coast of the United States. She'd married while in Canada and had two children, but after a few years, she'd left both marriage and children and returned to France.

Nicole's family was Algerian. She was a large woman with a booming voice, dark eyes and cropped, brown-mixed-with-gray hair. Openly lesbian, she wore her sexual preference proudly. Nicole was knowledgeable and competent with household repairs, carpentry, plumbing, and cars. She told me she'd long ago decided if a man could do something, she could do it, too. Her size and demeanor hid a heart of gold and a fragile psyche. She'd go out of her way to help anyone and was often hurt when others did not exhibit the same degree of kindness to her. Nicole had a small dog, a Lhasa Apso named Shona, a cute ball of salt-and-pepper fur. I really appreciated adding them to my group of French friends. My French "family" was growing.

I was reluctant even to think about leaving, but it was inevitable. Each day I did a little packing and started organizing the house to turn it back over to Gary. Just as spring was arriving, it was time for me to leave.

On departure day I tugged the heavy door closed and locked it. It had been repaired, but it required an effort to pull it firmly closed. I headed to Christine's Bakery to leave the key, where Gary would pick it up later in the week. Ah, the joys of village life! Just leave the house key at the bakery.

24 Parallels

FROM THE VINEYARDS AND CHERRY ORCHARDS of the Luberon to the vineyards and cherry orchards of Northern Michigan. Time to put on my Traverse City persona. Was it much different than the one I wore in France? I never really stopped to think about the parallels in my two worlds. Yes, even the word "parallel" was a connection, because Saignon and Leelanau County Michigan were both located on the 45th parallel. Was that why I felt such a connection?

April 29, 2010

Back at Woodmere Cottages. During the train ride to Paris, I saw miles and miles of bright-yellow fields. I was traveling later in the year than usual, so had never seen these blossoms before. The view was a granny's quilt of emerald and gold. I later looked it up and learned it was rapeseed in bloom. The plant makes vegetable oil. What a sight it was!

ALTHOUGH MELISSA WAS LIVING in her own house now, she offered to pick me up at Cherry Capital Airport. Beemer and Snowy would stay with her a few more days until I was settled. I had a nice, hot shower in *my* bathroom and a supper of quiche and salad that Melissa had purchased for me at Oryana Natural Foods

Market. I smiled. Quiche. She must have known I didn't want to feel too disconnected from France just yet.

Since the cats were with Melissa, I spent my first weekend with Joe, Sally, and Will. "Okay you guys, here you go." I started hauling out bags and packages from my typical French straw market basket. "And when it's empty, you can keep the basket. I have several I left with my stuff over there."

Over the years, I'd always brought back "goodies" from France. After the first few years, Joe, Sally, and I stopped shipping Christmas gifts. The postage was horrendous, and you never knew when the customs guys would hammer you with duty fees for sending (or receiving) items from abroad. I'd discovered Duty Free at the airport might be duty free, but it didn't necessarily mean cheaper. I'd opted to pick up gifts during the winter instead: a beaded key ring from the market, a nice scarf, likewise from the market, and to add to Joe's larder for food preparation, packages of *herbes de provence*.

Sally happily sniffed the bottle of lotion I'd handed to her. "You and I like the same kinds of fragrances, Jo Anne; this is perfect."

"Oh great, thanks," Joe said, as he hauled out a big square block of soap. The traditional *savon de Marseille* was his favorite. "I use this for everything," he went on. "I've got one in the laundry room for spots on clothes, and there's a piece in the kitchen for quick cleanups."

"Okay," he continued, "should we head to Frankfort and The Dinghy for fish and chips?" Sally took Will outside for a quick "doggy duty," and we piled into the car. Will loved to ride in the car and would wait there patiently while we enjoyed our supper, knowing we'd save a few tidbits for him.

It was a half-hour drive south to Frankfort located on the shore of Lake Michigan. When Joe and I were kids coming up north with our parents, the lighthouse and breakwater surrounded by a white-sand beach had been a vacation stop. The town had grown touristy but had character and charm. Boats, large and small, regularly came into the harbor off Lake Michigan, and it was home to a U.S. Coast Guard station. The breakwater along the harbor was a popular fishing spot. As much as I loved the mountain hills of the Luberon, I really missed being near a body of water. True, it was only an hour and a half from Saignon to Marseille and the Mediterranean, but they say in Michigan you are never more than five miles away from a lake or a river.

The Dinghy Restaurant was something of a legend in Frankfort and one of our go-to spots. For years, it had been a rough-and-tumble biker bar. New owners took over, and gradually it became more of a restaurant than a bar. Its nautical theme highlighted the history of the ferryboat fleet, which had steamed out of Frankfort harbor for ninety years, ending in 1982. Old car-ferry signs, taken from the pilothouses of ferryboats sailing between the harbors of Michigan, Indiana, Illinois, and Wisconsin, now hung from the ceiling. Beautiful handcrafted stained-glass windows above the entry continued the theme. The Friday night fish and chips meal was excellent fare and reasonably priced.

In summer, tourists rubbed elbows with the more elite residents who frequented Crystal Downs Country Club on the edge of town. You got there early, or else you waited up to an hour for a table.

Since we were reasonably early, we didn't have long to wait. "The usual?" Joe asked, looking at Sally and me.

"Works for me," I replied, and Sally nodded agreement.

"Fish and chips," Joe relayed to the waitress. "A mix of cod and walleye."

We sipped draft beers while waiting for our meal. I looked around the room and across the table. Why had I stayed away from this for so long? The company and the location were so familiar, so comfortable. Our dinner delivered, we enjoyed.

"Don't forget to save a piece of fish for Will," Sally reminded. I quickly broke off a piece of cod and wrapped it in a napkin. Declining dessert, we paid the bill, went to the car, and drove home.

That night, lying in their downstairs guest room, I thought about how good it felt to be with Joe and Sally hanging out at The Dinghy. I mused over the history associated with Frankfort, shipping, the Great Lakes. Yes, this history paled when compared to the history surrounding me in France, but it felt great to be here.

Sunday, after a perfect family weekend, I returned to Traverse

City. I went to bed early, feeling the effects of my recent travel, the time difference, and the strong emotions. I wanted to be here, with my family, but I wanted to be in France with my friends. How to resolve this conflict? Once again, I heard my Dad's voice, "You should be twins."

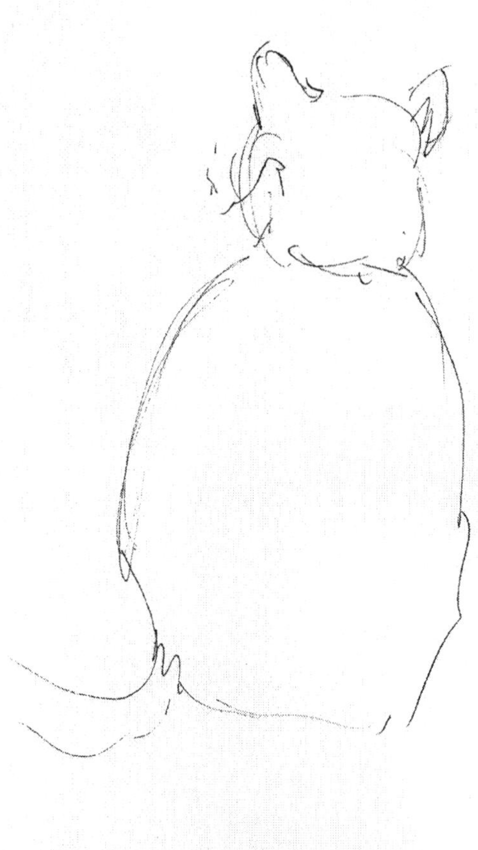

MONDAY, I WENT TO GET THE CATS. Melissa's house wasn't far from my Woodmere condo, and it was a quick and easy transition. The cats were happy and healthy and quickly resumed their condo habits. They sat in the window and stared at the birds or curled up on the afghan on the back of the sofa.

The cats were happy, but I wasn't. The good feelings from Frankfort did not last, and it didn't take long for condo crap to surface. As we moved toward summer and gardening, one couple complained the snow removal crew had wrecked the shrubs in front of their unit last winter. Perpetually perky Peggy, our association secretary, was doing a half-assed job of keeping track of things. Perky and energetic did not necessarily translate into efficient. She reminded me so much of Lizzie … scatty. Didn't anyone think to call the management company and have *them* contact the snow removal crew about the damages? Wasn't this the protocol decided upon at the last board meeting? It should be in the minutes, which were … where?

June 27, 2010

Back from overnight in Empire. Feeling much more relaxed. Joe and I went and bought strawberries at the roadside stand and we made two batches of jam. Joe grilled pork chops. Got an email from Saignon Sally saying how pleased Gary was with my stay last winter and looking forward to the next.

EVEN AS I ENJOYED FAMILY TIME, my mind was planning for the coming winter and my return to France. Although I was set to stay at Gary's house, my exact departure date was up in the air. I needed to be patient as I waited to hear when Gary planned to go back to New York and I could get into the Saignon house.

I'd spent time with Nicole and Brigitte last winter, often going to Goult to walk with them and Shona. Brigitte's house had a studio apartment on the lower level, and in April, before I'd left to come back to the States, she'd offered to have me come and stay in the fall. With my return date undecided, I had yet to confirm any plans to do so. I needed to decide what to do.

But, before I could make any plans, I needed to find a house sitter for the coming winter. It was already July. Departure date? Stay with Brigitte? House sitter? I had a trio of loose ends on my hands.

I ran an ad on MindMyHouse.com for a house sitter and got a reply from a young couple living in Canada. Originally, he'd lived in the Traverse City area and wanted to come back to finish his teaching degree at the college. I was a little wary of taking someone so unknown, but they furnished impeccable references from a local minister. We communicated via email and phone, and I sent them a house-sitting contract. The house-sitter hurdle was behind me … one down.

It was now late August, and I hadn't decided exactly on my departure date or what to do about Brigitte's studio apartment in Goult. Two to go.

As I struggled with my finances, I had been ignoring one option. Could I collect Social Security from either one of my two ex-husbands, now both deceased? I knew the law said if you'd been married for ten years, you were entitled to spousal benefits. Both marriages qualified, but just.

I'd been reluctant to investigate my options. I'd divorced them both. I didn't need them. But now I needed their money? Facing financial realities, I decided the idea was worth investigating and went to the local Social Security office. The helpful staff crunched some numbers, which showed I was entitled to collect from my first husband, the dentist. I needed to provide copies of our marriage license and divorce papers.

I had nigglings of pride, but then thought about how I had scrimped and scraped so he could go to dental school. We'd lived off the GI Bill and my teaching salary. I'd learned to make one little chicken last for three meals: roast it; then leftover creamed chicken on toast; and, finally, the bones … chicken soup. I decided I could accept his money. I'd earned it.

I finalized house-sitting arrangements with the Canadian couple, Brandon and Jodi, who would arrive in Traverse City and stay with friends until I left. In as much as they would be in town, there was no reason for me to delay going to France. I emailed Brigitte and told her I'd be delighted to use her studio apartment for the month of October. Three down.

Joe's birthday fell on the Saturday of Labor Day weekend, and I went to their house for the day to celebrate. He had a new bus route, and we took a dry run to Glen Arbor so he could estimate how long it would take him from his house to pick up his first student. Sally was coming down with a cold and was resting. Her normally twinkling, brown eyes were watering and red. She was a teacher and needed all of her energy to face a new batch of students. Joe and I took Will for a walk in between rain showers. We had cake and ice cream, watched a little TV, and I headed to Traverse City early.

September 28, 2010

I had a super weekend with Joe and Sally. Said good-bye. I took the cats to Melissa this morning, so they are settled. Am feeling a little stressed, think it's the added preps for the house sitters, but I'll manage. Took the car to the storage garage, and he brought me back. Fantastic news from Social Security. I'm getting $373 a month more!! I am so grateful.

I LOOKED FORWARD to a month with Brigitte, Nicole, and little Shona. Another dog to walk and added time with French friends.

October 1, 2010 Chez Brigitte - Goult

….Sitting beside the pool …finally in France. Shona is lying beside me. The trip was long, but uneventful. Mireille picked me up and left me with a few provisions. I had a nice supper with Nicole and Brigitte. Mireille and Jean-Claude came this morning with my suitcase of clothes. Later I'll walk up to the village with Brigitte and pick up a few groceries from the little épicerie. The internet wireless is up and running and works perfectly. So good to be here!

IT WAS A NEW VILLAGE, new surroundings, and living closer to people I didn't know very well. The bedroom/living area of the apartment had a low ceiling and reminded me of the guest room at Joe and Sally's. I spent a lot of time upstairs with Brigitte, Nicole, and Shona. Shona was a walking machine, and we walked every day.

If you stopped along the way to chat or look at something, she'd get impatient and bark at you to hurry up. I had to smile. Somehow, I'd acquired quite a cadre of dogs to walk: Will, Miel, and now Shona.

Living there, I became aware of challenges in Brigitte and Nicole's relationship and became something of a sounding board for complaints. They had different attitudes about life's responsibilities, like paying bills and saving money. I liked both of them and did not want to be in the middle. I just listened.

Brigitte and Nicole became true friends, my second French family. I didn't want to find myself living in France but isolated from the French. There was an inherent risk in getting caught up with the ex-pat-Anglo community. It was too easy to lapse into your own language and surround yourself with your compatriots.

November began chilly and wet. I did another few days of caring for the cats in Roussillon, which made a nice transition between my stay in the studio apartment in Goult to rue Cilly in Saignon. I was doing a bit of "village hopping," but the distances between lodgings were not very far. It was ten minutes from Goult to Roussillon and only twenty more to Saignon.

I got emails from Melissa updating me that my American cats were doing fine. House sitters Jodi and Brandon were going away for a week over the holiday, but Peggy said she'd keep an eye on the condo. From afar, I realized she really was a good neighbor, and I felt a twinge of guilt over my critical assessment of her behavior.

I spent a few days enjoying the company of Paul and Anne's cats and my spot on the sunny terrace looking over the valley toward the village of Lacoste and the nighttime lights of the chateau of the Marquis de Sade. I'd been taking care of Ellie, Sebby, and Frankie for a few years. I no longer had the sense of being somewhere new. And, it was nice to think that after the holidays, I'd be back for another stint of house and cat care, while Paul and Anne had a vacation.

WHEN PAUL AND ANNE RETURNED, I moved to Gary's house. He had suggested I come the night before he was to leave so we could review the heating system and go over any last-minute details. It poured rain on my drive, but I was thrilled to be able to park in my favorite spot on the quay. I quickly unloaded and took a suitcase up to "my" room.

"You'll remember the heating control box has two windows," Gary explained as we reviewed the system. "I've disconnected this circuit to the old dehumidifier, because I think it's what caused the fuses to blow last winter."

I glanced around the cave. The outer room was piled full of firewood Gary had ordered. "I'll get Mireille's son, Thomas, to come over and move some of this up to the garage," I said.

"Okay," he replied, "but be careful, because I have a car now, so don't pile the wood too close. Which reminds me, I've rigged up a charger for the car to keep the battery from running down. You'll need to connect it periodically. I'll show you how and then leave the directions." I shuddered. With Gary, nothing was ever straightforward and simple.

Later, Gary fixed a chicken curry accompanied by a bottle of wine from the cave. Sipping an after-dinner Calvados, we went over details. Email, we agreed, would quickly answer any questions that might arise. Gary left the next afternoon, and I was in charge.

Meg invited me to join them for Thanksgiving. Stephen's daughter, Maria, and her husband, Roger, were there. They both were working for American companies based in Germany. As usual, Meg outdid herself, and I contributed candied sweet potatoes, which went well with her turkey, stuffing, gravy, broccoli, and cranberry jelly.

Here I was, an American in France, celebrating another Thanksgiving. How many had this been? At the Claparèdes with Maureen and Joe. The year I'd invited Stephen and Elizabeth while I was house-sitting for Tim and Mary. A previous time here with Meg and Stephen. All good memories. I did have a few moments of nostalgia when I thought of Joe's Thanksgiving turkeys over the years, and the superb chestnut stuffing he made.

November 30—another birthday in France. Brigitte invited me for supper with them and suggested bringing my pajamas, so I wouldn't have to drive after dark nor worry about having a few glasses of wine. Supper was yummy with lamb, roasted potatoes, salad, cheese, and a gorgeous cake with a pear artfully drawn on the frosting. The French pastries never ceased to amaze me. Joe sent an email of birthday wishes, and I got cards from Paul, Anne, Meg, and Stephen. It was a very HAPPY birthday!

25 Holidays

AT CHRISTMAS, I always experienced a few pangs of … not exactly homesickness … but more than fleeting wishes that I were in Michigan. The holiday always evoked reminiscences of childhood and family. I had fond memories of Joe and Sally coming to my house in Glen Arbor, where we'd decorated the tree and taken long walks along the frozen, sandy beaches of Lake Michigan. On Christmas Eve, Joe baked the traditional "pigs in the blanket" our mother always made. It was a meatloaf mixture rolled inside a sweet homemade bread dough and baked. We always ate them cold with eggnog as we opened presents Christmas morning. I yearned for a true feeling of family in France and time with Mireille as well as Nicole and Brigitte fell short.

So much of French holiday tradition was steeped in its long history of Roman Catholicism. The more commercial side of Christmas had managed to creep into French life, but it was basically a religious holiday.

With the approach of Christmas and the New Year, a barrage of invitations to ex-pat drinks parties began. I had a tough time getting my head around the incessant need to party, party, party. It didn't have anything to do with Christmas, although Christmas was ostensibly the reason for a party. It became a contest to see whose invitations got sent out first, and which party managed to attract the most guests. I kept my head down and managed to accept one or two invitations, lest I be thought anti-social. But I much preferred the family-type celebrations such as the Christmas meal I'd enjoyed with Mireille and Jean-Claude's family.

My French friends erected a crèche, or "manger scene," as I was raised calling it, in a prominent location in their house. They did have a Christmas tree, but the traditions were mostly "the reason for the season" and leaned heavily on family and religion. I focused on the things I enjoyed: the lights in Apt, the images of candy canes, and memories of midnight mass with my father … and, if French churches had become pretty empty in modern times, they were filled at Christmas.

During the holiday, I had another stay at Paul and Anne's while they visited family in England. From the twenty-second of December until the twenty-ninth, I moved to Roussillon and had the company of the cats. I was happy when Brigitte invited me to come to their house in Goult for Christmas supper with her and Nicole.

December 26, 2010

A super Christmas Day! I got my bûche de Noël from Mireille Christmas Eve. I did small stuffed tomatoes and ham roll ups and took them and the bûche over to Goult around 1 p.m. Shona and I went for a walk up through the village. A relaxed afternoon and nice meal with my second French "family."

ON THE TWENTY-NINTH, Paul phoned to let me know they were on their way and would be back in time to feed the cats their supper. I gathered my things and returned to Saignon. Miracle of miracles, my favorite parking spot on the quay was open.

January 1, 2011 New Year's Day

Slept in. Didn't quite stay up until midnight but was faintly aware of hearing fireworks. A new year! New beginnings! Wonder where I'll be in January 1, 2012? Here? Perhaps.

I HAD A SUPER NEW YEAR'S DAY. I spent time organizing calendars and working on my goals in my journal. In the afternoon, I walked around the village and took some photos. I wrapped up in my shawl and sat on the terrace and read for at least an hour. Great fresh vitamin D! I loved the solitude and calm and wondered what it said about where I wanted to be? Could I let go of "winter in the Luberon"?

26 A Visitor

JANUARY SLOGGED ALONG. There were times when we were socked in with fog and mist, but when I thought of northern Michigan snowstorms, I could easily deal with a little fog. Most days there was sun, and I could sit on the terrace. I was sitting there one day when I had a thought. Here I was in this big house with three bedrooms, three bathrooms, and lots of living area. I wondered if Melissa could leave her counseling practice long enough to come for a visit?

I sent Melissa an email suggesting March would be a great time to visit. It would be warming up, pre-tourist season, so airfares would be more reasonable. (They were never cheap.) Melissa was eager to come, but she needed to sort out her work schedule before she could make any definite plans. Brandon and Jodi had taken care of the cats a couple of times when Melissa was away for a few days, so she'd check with them about the cats.

January 8, 2011

It's warm, 10C. Big news … Melissa is coming! Got what I needed at the supermarket yesterday. Brigitte and Nicole are coming for lunch with Shona tomorrow.

IN MID-JANUARY, Anne invited me to join them for a walk on the cliffs above a small village north of Roussillon. Back at their house, we had a yummy Niçoise salad with a bottle of rosé while sitting on the terrace in our shirtsleeves. Sitting outside in January! Just another reminder of why I was here and NOT back in Michigan.

My cat buddy, Sebastian, was closed up in the bedroom. He'd had a biopsy on his ear. Being a white cat in the sunshine of Provence had its disadvantages. He'd developed some nasty-looking growths on his ears, and the vet wanted to check them out.

MELISSA ARRANGED HER WORK schedule and cat care with Brandon and Jodi. I could now do an E-Ticket for the train, which was so much more convenient than how I'd always had my own tickets mailed to Meg, who would then send them on to me.

I looked forward to sharing my adopted country. I did *so* want everyone to love France, Provence, the Vaucluse, and the Luberon … just as much as I did.

January 23, 2011

Went to market in Apt yesterday and picked up some veggies. I stopped at the Royals café, where the ex-pat group gathers but did not stay long. I was embarrassed by the loud laughter and talking. The same thing happened earlier this week at the Aptois café. There seems to be a need to be "noticed" and "recognized" as someone important … "regulars." This week I move to Roussillon, a nice change of scene and the company of Ellie, Frankie, and Sebby. Tomorrow the vet gives the results of the biopsy on Sebby's ear.

AT THE END OF JANUARY, I went to Roussillon and spent three weeks with my cat buddies, while Paul and Anne went on vacation. The vet said the growths on Sebby's ear were malignant. Paul and Anne talked and included me, which I appreciated. We all concurred cutting off most of Sebby's ear just did not seem right. He was such a proud little guy. We thought it might damage him psychologically, so we decided to take a wait-and-see approach.

In the midst of planning for Melissa's visit and worry about Sebby, I got some assurance from Gary that I could have the Saignon house for the winter of 2011-2012 … exact dates and rent to be determined. Yippee!

I concluded my three-plus weeks of cat care in Roussillon, and it was time to gear up for Melissa's visit.

"MELISSA," I CALLED OUT. "Over here." I'd been up onto the platform when the train came in but didn't see her get off. I hurried back down to the lobby area, and there she was, standing by the magazine shop.

"Oh, Jo Anne," she said, giving me a big hug. "I'm so happy to be here! What a long trip! And I goofed when I printed out my train ticket. I printed the receipt and not the actual ticket, and the conductor was really cross with me. He scribbled something on the paper and said I needed to check at the station."

"Don't worry about it," I assured her. If he didn't demand you pay right there on the spot, you're off the hook. "You sure travel light,"

I said as I grabbed her small suitcase. She shouldered her backpack, and we headed to the car.

As we drove through Apt, I pointed out the supermarkets and other spots I'd mentioned in emails. We crossed town and took the winding road up to Saignon. "Look up, Melissa," I said. "See that big rock against the sky? That's Saignon, and our house is just below it."

Melissa admired the view as I made the ten-minute drive up the winding road. I rounded the final, sharp curve and drove up the quay toward the house. "Oh my gosh!" Melissa exclaimed. "Look! Forsythia in bloom." There was, indeed, a bush next to the road in yellow splendor. Having left heaps of snow and gray skies in Michigan, it was a real surprise for her to see blossoms in March. My favorite parking spot was open. I parked the car, we grabbed her gear, and climbed the steps to the front door.

"This is it!" I announced proudly. "Rue Cilly, my home in Saignon."

I wanted Melissa to meet everyone and to see first hand the things I'd told her about and loved in my adopted country. We didn't hang out exclusively with the ex-pats, and I was pleased to discover Melissa spoke and understood a little French. Who knew? I'd never asked, and she'd never offered. I took her to meet Mireille and Jean-Claude, where we drank tea and conversed in a mix of French and English. They were impressed with her and her French. We went to Goult to visit Brigitte and Nicole and took Shona for a walk.

The two of us enjoyed the markets, strolling among the stalls, and bought wine at a local winery. One Tuesday, we joined Meg's group on a hike down into the valley below the tiny village of Buoux. I had a fleeting thought of the year I had transported the uninvited cats from the Claparèdes to this locale. Over the years, I'd developed a real affinity for this quaint village and its valley lined with fields of lavender. There was something about it; every time I went there, it drew me in. Whenever I visited Buoux, I had this weird feeling … as if I'd been here in the past. It was an odd sensation, and one I couldn't explain. Déjà vu? A past life?

I'd discovered Buoux that first year I stayed at the Claparèdes. I was driving around, exploring, and turned off the main road on a whim. There was a quaint restaurant where I'd often go for a meal. It was like eating in the household dining room. Food was served family style and was authentically Provençal. You had to call and order a day ahead of time if you wanted the *plat du jour*. Otherwise, you could always have a scrumptious *Omelette Provençal,* a tossed salad slathered in olive oil, and a lot of garlic. The restaurant eventually closed, and I missed it.

Returning from the walk in Buoux, we drove past the Domaine des Claparèdes, and I noticed the gates were open. I backed up the car and went in. Lizzie and Andrew had divorced, and in the settlement Lizzie retained ownership of their house, the Lantins, on the other side of Saignon from the Claparèdes. Andrew got the Domaine and had promptly sold it.

The new owners, a German couple, were working that day. I'd met them on a previous occasion, and they graciously allowed me to show Melissa the property I'd once called home. It was such a pleasure to have her see the buildings and the views, but most of all it was a pleasure to see the improvements the Germans were making. The houses and property looked fantastic. New paint, new windows, gardens weeded, and although it was only mid-March, the swimming pools were glistening with fresh water.

Back in Saignon, we walked around the village and climbed the steps on the walls of the old chateau to the top of the rock, which overhangs the village. In all the years I'd been visiting, I'd never screwed up enough courage to climb to the top of the rock. I did not like heights, but with Melissa ahead of me, I braved the stairs and shared the magnificent view. Later, we sat in the sun on the terrace and grilled chicken for supper.

The days melted like a snowman in spring and it was time for her to head back to Michigan. The next day, I drove her to Avignon and she boarded the TGV to Charles De Gaulle. I'd arranged for her to stay overnight at the airport, making it easy to catch a plane the next morning.

27 Surprises, Bureaucracy, and Sadness

WITH SPRINGTIME, village activity picked up, and I started wishing I could stay longer, even a full year. I wanted another year like the one I had in Mary and Tim's house followed by Meg and Stephen's apartment. Could I find a place to rent I could afford? Should I just be happy with the current back-and-forth arrangement? After all, five or six or sometimes seven months a year in Provence was not bad. Then Gary sent an email saying he wasn't coming over until early May. I didn't need to leave in April; I could stay longer.

March 23, 2011

A miracle! I was able to change my plane ticket to leave May 11th. It'll cost me $253. Then Anne emailed that they want me to stay through the 15th and take care of the cats so they can go to Sweden for a sporting event, and they'd help pay for my ticket changes. I emailed Melissa and she's OK to keep the cats for the extra weeks.

IN APRIL, Stephen suddenly decided he wanted to move back to the States; to Charleston specifically, where his daughter Maria and her husband Roger would live after their time in Germany. Meg was aghast. They'd moved to France twenty years ago. Meg's sister was in England, but her life and friends were in the Luberon.

I wondered about Stephen's health. His ability to speak French had never moved beyond rudimentary. I thought about an Australian friend who'd left France to go back to Australia. "When you get old," he'd told me, "it's easier to be sick in your own language."

Was this Stephen's thinking?

He had a history of making major decisions on his own and then announcing them to Meg. She had told me when they were living in London: He was working as a stockbroker, and came home one evening to announce he'd turned in his notice. He was retiring. Not much collaboration in that relationship.

Then there was another upset for a couple I was so close to, when Nicole and Brigitte decided to split up. They'd been living together in Brigitte's house, but now Nicole found a tiny but charming cabanon to rent in the country between Roussillon and Goult. I did my best to remain neutral. When I was with Nicole, all she did was go on and on about Brigitte's faults ... she was careless with money, she lacked motivation, and so it went. When I was with Brigitte, she complained about Nicole's loud voice, her personal habits, and inability to relax.

These people had become my friends, part of my extended family in France, and it pained me to see them unhappy. The best I could do was lend a sympathetic ear and try not to take sides. I had my own concerns. It was time to file for the annual renewal of my *Carte de Séjour*. This was the identity card allowing me to stay in France longer than the three months permitted with only a passport.

I'd applied for my first *Carte* in 2004 when I came to take over the Claparèdes property for Lizzie and Andrew. The initial process was onerous at best. It involved getting a long-stay visa from the French government. After supplying requisite, copious documentation and fees, I'd had to fly to Chicago to the French Consulate and obtain the visa in person. Once I got to France, I had a limited number of days to apply for my *Carte* at the local Mairie in Saignon, and the process was no less arduous.

I needed a photo ID and proof of sufficient income to support myself. This meant documentation from the local bank stating I had an account in good standing. Yes, I was contributing to the economy. Since I was using my married name of Wilson, I had to supply a copy of my divorce decree, which I assumed was a vestige of the country's ingrained Catholicism. I was reminded … bureaucracy IS a French word. The renewal process was somewhat less complicated but involved letters and the payment of fees. Several years later, it necessitated going to the Préfecture in Avignon. No more messing around with the local Mairie.

As I prepared to leave for the summer, I had to be sure the paperwork was filed. This requirement contributed in no small way to my annual spring search for next winter's lodging. When I filed for my *Carte*, even the renewal, I had to provide proof of domicile. I asked Gary if he would be willing to provide this year's letter and he agreed. Just sending the letter did not suffice, because I had to provide a copy of Gary's passport and recent electric bill, which proved he was who he said he was and owned the place he was offering for me to live in.

Over the years, I'd learned that an electric bill from EDF, *Electricité de France*, the state-owned electric company, was a valuable piece of paper. It proved you were who you said you were and lived where you said you lived. I got the impression that when you died in France, and arrived at the Pearly Gates, if you could show St. Peter your EDF bill, he'd wave you in.

I got a copy of the bill from Gary, so I could tick this box off on the list and put it with my papers to file. Deadlines were deadlines, and I had to get my request filed before I left. I would pick up the *Carte* when I returned the following fall.

Maria and Roger were visiting Meg and Stephen, and Meg invited me to join them all for supper. It was good having Maria and Roger there, because Stephen was going into the hospital on Monday for a heart catheterization. Since they'd be at the hospital, I told Meg I'd go down, feed Miel, and take her for a walk

During dinner conversation, it became apparent Stephen was being forced to think about the ramifications of moving back to the

States, not the least of which was health care. When he'd retired, he'd dropped the company health insurance. In France, he was completely covered by being married to Meg, a Brit, with Britain being part of the European Union. I thought the family had been talking to him about pre-existing conditions and the state of health care insurance in the States. Maybe he'd change his mind. Meg sure hoped so, because she had no intention of moving to the United States.

Then I got a distressing email from Melissa. Snowy had suddenly gotten very sick. She'd taken him to the emergency vet service, and they'd diagnosed kidney failure. I called and talked to the female vet who was very kind and understanding, but also firm in saying nothing could be done. I felt sorry that Melissa was left to handle it, but the cats had become as much hers as mine, and I knew the little guy would be comforted having her with him when the vet administered the shot.

I was devastated about the loss and cried off and on for days. I'd be back in Michigan in less than a week, but Snowy would be gone.

I packed and sorted and cleaned and cleared. I had periods when I'd think of Snowy, and start crying. I took a suitcase over to Mireille to put in storage and mailed one last box of belongings. I got all my papers filed for the *Carte de Séjour*. I visited with the neighbors in the village and said my good-byes. It was heartwarming when they said how happy they were that I'd be back in the fall. Paul and Anne called to say how sorry they were to hear I'd lost Snowy. They were cat lovers. They understood.

Departure day, I tugged the front door shut, pocketed the key, and left it at Christine's bakery. Gary would retrieve it when he arrived later in the week.

28 Revolving Door

I COULD NEVER GET USED to the rapidity with which I was yanked out of one life and culture and plopped down into another. Two days ago, I'd dropped my suitcases and my car with Mireille and Jean-Claude, and a high-speed train ride later I was at the airport in Paris. The next morning, I was on a jet USA bound. My body got transported quickly, but it always took longer for my mind and spirit to catch up. I sighed. I was back in Michigan, but my heart was in France.

Melissa had, again, picked me up at Cherry Capital Airport. She'd purchased a freshly roasted chicken, salad, and fruit for my supper. We chatted a while and cried over Snowy. After I dumped my suitcase upstairs, I poured a glass of wine, sat down, and looked around. The condo looked fine. I'd arranged to have the cleaning lady come in after Brandon and Jodi left, so things were neat and tidy. I called Joe and Sally to let them know I'd made it, had a quick shower, my supper, and tumbled into bed. It seemed odd not to have the cats. Beemer was with Melissa. Snowy was gone.

The next afternoon, I saw my neighbor Rod out walking and was shocked at how frail he looked. I thought back to that day when he and I had met at Office Max, and he brought me to see what would become "Woodmere Cottages" and my home.

DESPITE HAVING TO CONFRONT Snowy's death, it was comforting to come back to Michigan when the last of winter's snow and slush had melted. It wasn't as much of a jolt coming from the blossoming Luberon. Here, trees were just beginning to leaf out, but the tulips were in bloom.

I'd planned to get Beemer from Melissa's house, and she invited me to come for supper. We shared a glass of wine and shed more tears over the loss of Beemer's buddy, Snowy. They'd been together fifteen years. Beemer looked good, but he was showing signs of his sixteen years. After supper, I brought out the package I'd put aside.

"Oh, Jo Anne, they're perfect!" Melissa exclaimed as she unfolded the linen dishtowels. "And look, this one's even got a recipe on it for ratatouille."

"I thought of you the minute I saw it," I replied. "The picture of the eggplant and peppers are so vivid. I figured it would go well with your kitchen."

I was feeling jet lagged, and Melissa had counseling clients the next day, so I didn't stick around. We gathered Beemer's cat toys and food, then loaded him into his little carrier. He'd always been good about being transported around, and after an initial mew of complaint, he settled in for the short ride to Woodmere.

The following Sunday I visited Joe and Sally. We did what had become the ritual unpacking of goodies from France. "Oh, good," Joe exclaimed, "You got another big bar of the Marseille soap. My other one is about gone."

"Joe, these are not to be used to wipe up barbeque sauce," Sally admonished, as she pulled out dishtowels similar to those I'd gotten for Melissa. He replied with an eye roll. We enjoyed grilled steaks and asparagus while talking about the winter and how I had adjusted to my second year of living in the village.

The summer of 2011 could be described in a couple of words— fitness and frustration. After checking out several gyms around town, I settled on one called Fit for You. It was too far to walk, but just a little over a five-minute drive. I signed up for sessions with a personal trainer and took advantage of the exercise classes, which included the new craze, Zumba. I'd always loved to dance, and the Zumba classes suited me perfectly.

Fit for You saved my sanity that summer. I would go for training sessions and classes, but I'd also often pop over for a few miles on the treadmill and work with the weight machines. I pared my size-twelve jeans down to a comfy size-ten and my emotions over losing Snowy and missing France from turmoil to almost tranquil.

AFTER FITNESS, THERE WAS FRUSTRATION, coming largely from renewed condo crap. Neighbor Peggy became an increasingly loose cannon. She'd swoop down on me the first thing in the morning with complaints about the management company and our co-owners. She had no sense of organization or business, and I ultimately got into a shouting match with her over how the irrigation system should be working.

Did I need this? I wanted fields of lavender and air filled with its fragrance and the buzzing of bees, not soggy, overwatered lawn, and a busybody neighbor.

July 5, 2011

I've been looking at ads in the paper for apartment rentals around town. Rod came over to chat a little. He's in sad shape. I do not want to end up that way. Got two emails from Nicole in France, with cute photos of Shona.

BY MID-JULY, my frustration worsened, and I knew I had to find a place where I could feel settled. (Although I continued to seriously wonder what that feeling would be like. What and where was "home"?) I decided to have some improvements done on the condo and put it up for sale. I did not know where I'd go, but I was willing to put up with uncertainty in order to get out from under the emotional and financial demands of owning a house. I called the realtor who'd sold my Glen Arbor house.

"Rob, it's Jo Anne Wilson. How's business?" I asked.

"Hey, Jo Anne, good to hear from you. How was France?" came the reply.

"It was great; in fact so good, I want to spend even more time over there before I'm too old or can't afford to do it. I want to sell this condo; do you want the listing?"

"Absolutely," he answered, "What's your timeline?"

"I'm having the upstairs bathroom floor re-done, and once that's finished, I'm good to go," I came back.

"It sounds good. I'll do some research on condo properties on the market, and you give me a call when you're ready."

I hung up the phone and immediately felt better. That same week, I began looking at apartments in and around Traverse City. Oh boy, I thought … my perpetual quest for where I was going to live next.

As the days passed, I was discouraged and saddened watching my neighbor, Rod, go into a physical downward spiral for which he was ultimately hospitalized. When he got out, I helped as I could by visiting and taking over soup and casseroles for meals.

Later that month, Rod was diagnosed with congestive heart failure and went back into the hospital. This time, when he got out, he was moved into a long-term health care facility in Frankfort. The sight of his dark condo was depressing. I remembered our initial visit when I'd decided I wanted to live here, and the first year when I'd moved in, he and I had been the only residents. He'd been gone to his farm a lot in summers past, but this was different. I had the feeling he'd never come back to Woodmere Cottages. He'd been my anchor there, and his absence was heartbreaking, but it somehow made it easier for me to think of letting go of the condo.

Late in July, I phoned Meg. We had a nice, long chat, but it didn't help my morale. Things were not any more settled on her side of the ocean than on mine. There was no resolution to Stephen's maladies; he had a heart condition, was on new medication, and being monitored by a cardiologist. In keeping with his unilateral decision-making, he had called in a realtor and told Meg they were putting the house up for sale. She was distraught.

I'd contacted my handyman to work on condo updates. He re-did the upstairs bathroom with a tile floor and repaired the drywall around the back door, which had deteriorated. I went to Fit for You as often as I could, sometimes five days a week. Exercise helped reduce stress, or so they said.

August 11, 2011

The realtor came at noon, and the condo is officially listed. The neighbors who have been so unhappy came over, and they are putting their unit back on the market. So that's two. Ideally, I wish mine were the only one, but so be it.

OVER THE ENSUING WEEKS, I got calls saying a realtor had a client and wanted to show my condo. I became pretty adept at stashing Beemer's litter box and toys in a closet, then loading him into his carrier. The two of us drove around until the showing was over. I was grateful he was such a good little cat, because his buddy, Snowy, never liked being in the car and would complain non-stop whenever he had to be transported anywhere. I was missing that ball of snowy fur, and I think Beemer was, too. As for the condo showings, I got lots of positive feedback, but no prospective buyer.

The beginning of September was Labor Day weekend and Joe's birthday, so I went to their house for the day to celebrate. The weather was gorgeous, which meant we could sit on the back deck facing the woods, while Joe grilled ribs in the yard.

After lunch we drove into Glen Arbor for ice cream. The village was packed with tourists, and as I looked around, I was surprised to see how much things had changed since I'd moved away in January 2004. Art's Tavern was still the hub of activity. Cherry Republic buzzed with people wanting ice cream and cherry pie. I'd had a good thirteen years in Glen Arbor but did not regret having moved on. It looked familiar, but I felt strangely detached. Had this really ever been a part of my life? I remembered how perfect it had felt when I first moved there. What had changed? There it was again, that repeated wondering, "Where I am supposed to be"? We bought ice cream and took it back to the house, where we had birthday cake on the deck. As the sun went down and the air began to cool, I said goodbye and went back to Beemer.

The following week, I got an email saying Rod had died. Sadness poured over me as I thought of him spending his last days in a care facility. He'd always been so independent and would have hated relying on other people. He hadn't really planned for old age or illness. It jolted me. I wasn't getting any younger. I wanted more time in France, and maybe it was time to take steps to make that dream a reality while I had good health and, with some budgeting, could afford it. Another year in Provence for me? Why not!

There were several more condo showings in September, but no offers. I was due to leave for France on November 18, and was in a quandary about the condo sale. I really did not want to deal with it long distance. The realtor held an open house, which was well attended, but nothing came of it. Always the optimist, I put a deposit on an apartment in a nearby complex. If the condo sold, I'd have time to move.

Selling the condo was on the table, so I decided not to seek a house sitter for the winter. For a reasonable fee, my handyman would come by and check on things every week. I knew the neighbors would also keep an eye open. In spite of the irritations, there was some advantage to having close neighbors.

November arrived and along with it, my countdown to departure. I did a last-minute cleanup of leaves in my front garden and also those in Rod's gardens. His condo was sitting dark and empty, and I felt sad whenever I looked across the courtyard.

I was leaving on a Friday and the weekend before I went to Joe and Sally's so we could have an early Thanksgiving. Although it wasn't on Thanksgiving Day, it sure felt good to be celebrating the holiday on this side of the ocean, after so many years of a *faux* holiday in France.

We took a short walk through the woods and then settled into Joe's stuffed turkey and trimmings, including corn relish and green bean mushroom soup casserole, which our family traditionally ate on Turkey Day. We ended the meal with Sally's sweet potato pie.

The following Monday I took my condo off the market and withdrew the check on hold for a potential apartment rental. The week was full of last-minute wrap-up: pack the suitcase, clean the refrigerator, clear all the trash, and check the basement. I arranged to drop off my car for storage. Miraculously, it all got done, and it was departure day. *Au revoir Michigan, bonjour France.*

29 An Encore Winter in Saignon

November 19, 2011 Rue Cilly Saignon, France

I'm here, and in some ways, it feels as if I never left. Mireille and Jean-Claude met me at the train station in Avignon. Marcel brought the key, and by 8:00 PM, I was in. Suitcases are stacked in the other bedroom. Gary left a bottle of rosé in the fridge along with fresh fruit, bread, and cheese Sally and Marcel brought.

USUALLY I DIDN'T HAVE AS MUCH of a jet-lag problem at this end, as I did going the other direction, but this time was different. I was dragging. I needed to be on top of things. Thanksgiving was coming up, and I'd planned a birthday celebration for myself on the thirtieth of the month. This year was another milestone, seventy-five, and several weeks earlier I'd sent the invitations to my ex-pat Luberon friends. I don't know why I was reluctant to mix my French friends with the ex-pat group, but it didn't feel like a good fit.

I'd accepted an invitation for Thanksgiving "lunch" from Laurie, an American who'd moved permanently to France the year before. Laurie wasn't tall, in her early sixties, had short, brown, curly hair and dark eyes. There was nothing dainty about her or her no-nonsense, take-charge personality. She had an engineering background and had managed factories in Europe. Having lived and worked all over the U.S. and Europe, she'd settled in France with two close Brit friends. They had purchased and restored an enormous house on a hill above Apt, which they rented to vacationers. Since there were currently no renters in the Apt house, that was where our Thanksgiving lunch would take place.

It was a festive meal with turkey and all the usual trimmings. Laurie, Stephen, and I were the only Americans among the fifteen people at the table. There was champagne before the meal and lots of wine during. The day was pleasant, but I had lingering memories of the early Thanksgiving with Joe and Sally. This one felt contrived, and I couldn't help thinking about the mostly ex-pats attending and the irony of Brits celebrating a holiday established by the Pilgrims, who had come to America to escape religious persecution in England.

The day after Thanksgiving, I phoned Meg, and she mentioned she was not feeling well. I'd noticed, after we had eaten and were sitting around the table chatting, that she got up and went into the living area and sat on the sofa. I told her to call me if she needed anything, but she said she was fine. I wondered if worry over selling the house was making her unwell.

The following Saturday, I went to market and stopped at the café for the usual ex-pat gathering. It was the same: loud talk, loud laughter. I don't know why the atmosphere made me uncomfortable, but I felt like an outsider. I thought back to when I'd first been welcomed to the Saturday group. How good it had felt to "belong." What had changed? Them? Me?

MY EFFORTS TURNED to birthday-party planning, and a couple of days before the party, Marcel brought wine for the event. I was reminded it was because of Marcel and his American wife, Sally, that I'd met Gary, thus my current status as a resident of the village.

"Just put the boxes over there on the terrace, Marcel," I directed. "I really appreciate your help."

"Well, Jo Anne, I've been in the wine export business for a while, and I'm happy to do it. I got a case of white, a case of red, and a half case of rosé. People tend not to drink rosé this time of year, but I figured you could always store what isn't opened down in Gary's wine cave. There's plenty of room on the rack to the right of the doorway."

"Thank you so much, Marcel, this is really reasonable," I said, examining the bill and reaching for my wallet.

"The woman at the shop knows me, and since I was buying quite a lot, she gave me a good discount. We'll see you Wednesday night. Would you like us to come a little early to get set up?"

"Oh, that would be great," I assured him. "Sally offered to make some finger food, and Meg and Anne are bringing things as well. Will you take charge of the wine?"

Marcel assured me he'd be happy to serve the wine, and after he left, I looked at the bill again and did the math. He really had gotten a bargain. I was grateful, because I was watching my spending very carefully.

November 30 arrived, my birthday, and the weather was glorious. Evening came, and my guests wandered around the kitchen and dining/living area enjoying food and conversation. I felt extremely happy and fortunate to be surrounded by friends who were celebrating my birthday here in France.

December 1, 2011

The party went really well. There was plenty of food, and Anne and Sally each made a birthday cake with candles and all. There were 23 people.

DOING CLEANUP, the day after the party, I thought about my friends in France and the birthdays I'd spent here. Each time had been special in different ways … the year Mireille had come to the Claparèdes with cake, and then Maureen and Joe with a raspberry tart. Then, the Claparèdes birthday supper with Elizabeth, Meg, and Stephen, later my big seventieth party at Tim and Mary's house, then fettuccini alfredo with Stephen.

My life in my adopted country was developing its own history.

30 Facing Reality

WITH MY BIRTHDAY a happy memory, I began to focus on the days and months ahead. I was back in France where I'd thought I wanted to be, but I was having trouble turning off thoughts of stateside family. I had a long email from Joe, and he was really suffering with a bad back. Melissa emailed to say her best friend, Amy, was moving away. In some ways, as much as I wanted to be there, it was harder this time. I felt a lot of sadness—just the changes of life, I suspect, and, thinking of my recent birthday … instead of … age.

The following week, I got notification there would be a refund on my car insurance in Michigan, since the vehicle was in storage. The funds were welcomed, because Jean-Claude had purchased new tires for the Old Gray Mare, and I needed to pay him back.

December 14, 2011

Yesterday Meg called and wanted to come up with her computer. She was very angry with Stephen. The realtor had a showing scheduled, and Stephen was doing nothing to get ready. Just sitting on the sofa watching TV. Meg said he'd mentioned to Laurie that he's going to the States to visit Maria this winter. When she asked him about it, he denied it.

CHRISTMAS HOLIDAY SPIRIT was in full swing. Joe and Sally had decided to go to Mexico for Christmas. Will would go to the doggy spa, and they would escape to sun and sand. For several years, the three of us had gone to a small, family resort near Playa del Carmen on the Caribbean in Eastern Mexico. I suddenly wished I could be there with them. I shook off the longing and faced the reality of where I was and how I was going to celebrate Christmas. Brigitte had invited me for Christmas Day brunch, and since I'd be cat-sitting for Paul and Anne over the holiday, I'd be close by and accepted.

December 26, 2011

All in all, I had a nice Christmas Day. In the morning, I went to Mireille's and picked up the bûche de Noël she had made for me. I prepared deviled eggs and bacon-wrapped prunes to take for brunch. We had fresh oysters, smoked salmon roll stuffed with cheese, and roast chicken. After lunch, I walked with Brigitte, Nicole, and Shona.

THE WEEK FOLLOWING CHRISTMAS, I tried to ignore the hype over the upcoming New Year's Eve celebrations. Many of the restaurants had posted special menus for *Le Réveillon de Nouvel An*. I thought back to the years when I would have been right there, up to my elbows getting ready for confetti and balloons, but I simply no longer enjoyed those festivities.

Speaking with Meg on the phone, she confessed to not quite having recovered from her Thanksgiving malaise. It had dragged on for almost a month, and putting on the mulled wine party hadn't allowed her much time to rest. I stopped by to retrieve the dish from the goodies I'd taken to her party, and found her with a wracking cough and extreme fatigue. I wondered if it was partly caused by stress over Stephen's decision to put their house up for sale.

Paul and Anne returned on the twenty-ninth, and I was able to leave Roussillon for New Year's Eve in Saignon. In more recent years, I'd begun to think the beginning of a new year was a time for retrospection and introspection, and I celebrated *Le Réveillon de Nouvel An* my way: alone and quietly.

I was scheduled to go to Paul and Anne's again mid-January through the middle of February. After a couple of weeks to re-adjust from the holidays, I went back and started the new year with my cat buddies, Frankie, Ellie, and Sebby.

At the end of January, we had several days of extremely cold temperatures, and it snowed non-stop. The radio and TV did nothing but talk about the record-breaking weather. The bitterly cold temperatures created a real challenge for me, because Paul and Anne did not winterize their swimming pool. The pump circulating the water during the night was ordinarily sufficient to avoid freezing. Ordinarily, but not this time. Over the next few days, I went out repeatedly with a wooden-handled broom to break up the ice. I switched the pump from running periodically to running twenty-four hours a day and prayed.

Paul and Anne had given me the phone number of their very nice neighbor, a Frenchman who lived just up the lane. Mid-week I phoned him and he came and did some adjustments on the pool assuring me I really had nothing to worry about. Easy for him to say.

Marcel and Sally were checking on Gary's house in Saignon, which relieved me of that responsibility. After a few days of chopping up ice in the pool and watching the thermometer stay stuck in below-freezing numbers, I began to think wistfully of sunny Provençal blue skies and balmy temperatures. Again, I could hear myself smugly saying, "Oh, it may snow once or twice during the winter, but only an inch or so, and it always melts within a day." Bite my tongue.

> *February 2, 2012*
>
> *It's snowing again. I moved my car up closer to the road, but I'm in and comfy and no need to leave, even if I could get out. Melissa emailed and Beemer is doing fine. That's a relief. An automated message on the phone warning residents around Roussillon that pipes may freeze due to the severe cold. Oh boy!*

AFTER A WEEK, the weather eased up, and the snow melted. I was able to settle into my usual pattern of feeding the cats and enjoying sun on the terrace. Mid-February, Paul and Anne returned to Roussillon and I to Saignon.

31 More People and Pets

SHORTLY AFTER THE HOLIDAYS, Paul and Anne introduced me to another couple, Michael and Susan, who lived in the countryside east of Apt. Originally from England, they had made their home and life solidly in France for the past twenty years and had two cats. Michael had been a psychologist with a very successful career in England. He had rather long, wispy, blond-going-gray hair, which was fly away. His Brit-accented voice was soft. He had a slight build and a very deliberate, warm manner about him.

Susan was tall and slim. Her short-cut hair was light brown with some evidence of gray. Her accented voice and manner were friendly and welcoming, which made me think she'd been excellent at her profession as a social worker. She'd had her share of physical challenges, having had knee and hip replacements as well as a bout with breast cancer. None of this was in evidence as she maintained beautiful gardens around the house and thought nothing of clambering up a ladder to trim the gorgeous roses that climbed the trellises all around the property.

They wanted to go away the following October and asked me if I'd come and take care of the house and the cats. This would mean I could move up my usual November arrival, just as I had in Goult at Brigitte's studio apartment. I happily agreed to tack on the extra month. I couldn't quite be in France year-round, but I was doing my best to add weeks on to my regular schedule.

March 18, 2012

I went to Michael and Susan's for lunch, met the cats, and toured the house. They have a lovely apartment on an upper level in back of the house, so it's completely private. It does have a wood-burning stove, but it should not be a problem in October. I'll look forward to being there.

IT WAS TIME TO RENEW my *Carte de Séjour*, and Gary agreed, again, to provide the necessary documentation for my proof of residency. We talked about another winter, and the indications were all good for me to be in Saignon. I could relax without the niggling need to search for lodging. I retrieved the required letter from the bank, affirming my account in good standing. Yes, I was depositing money, spending it, contributing to the French economy, and trying desperately not to think about how weak the dollar was against the euro. All of my income was in dollars. All of my spending was in euros. Not a good combination.

For five months, I had pretended I lived here, but it was time to go … I had to face reality, and it was beginning to wear on me. I'd always prided myself on being flexible, able to adjust and adapt, but I was growing weary of trying to adapt to living in two different cultures. Why did I have to leave France! I had a month before leaving for Michigan, time to clear closets, cupboards, and pack, which was difficult for me emotionally.

There was no space or place to stow things, because Gary, Cathy, and summer visitors would utilize every inch of cupboards, cabinets, and closets (of which there were not a lot). Fortunately, Mireille and Jean-Claude were willing to store my things at their house, but it would have been so much easier if I hadn't had to pack the suitcases and cartons and haul them to Gargas … physically easier and emotionally less wrenching.

Mireille had gotten to be difficult to be around. She carried on incessantly about family problems. I couldn't have a conversation with her, because she wouldn't listen. She would rant and rave and talk non-stop. I didn't know if it was hormones or something more insidious, but I went out of my way to avoid calling her or going to visit. It was sad, because we had been close for so many years. Her family was my French family, but her behavior was starting to make me wish I'd never adopted them.

To add to my distress, I got news from my friends, Mary and Tim, saying that Tim had been diagnosed with bone cancer, and the prognosis wasn't good. Tim was such a big man; his robust size made it difficult for me to imagine him with a debilitating condition.

I thought back to taking care of their house in 2006-2007 while they'd gone to Australia. Here was another reminder of the importance of doing things while time is available and health is good! Tim's news reinforced my determination to find a way to spend more time in France. Was it time to drop the price on my condo to encourage a sale?

In late March, Meg invited me to join her, Stephen, Mary, and

Tim for supper. I hadn't seen a lot of Mary and Tim, but we'd kept in contact by phone and email.

"Hello there, come on in." Stephen beamed though his mustache and goatee as he gave me his usual bear hug and took my coat. "How are things up in the village?"

"Not bad at all," I replied. "A bit more activity now that the weather is better."

"Hi, Jo Anne," Meg called from the corner by the stove. "Stephen, pour us a glass of wine, please. I'll be done with this sauce in a minute. Mary phoned and said they'd be a little late, so we can have a drink while we wait."

We settled in the living room and sipped until Tim and Mary arrived. Stephen fixed a drink for them, and they joined us.

"I'm sure you've heard my news," Tim said. "At least I know why I've had such pain in my back for several months. I start my chemo and radiation next week."

I watched Mary's face as Tim talked about his diagnosis and treatment. Her already diminutive stature seemed to shrink as Tim spoke of his condition. I knew it was going to be as hard on her as it would be on him. He did, however, sound upbeat and positive.

I marveled at his attitude and made a mental note not to put off doing what I really wanted to do. People say there are no guarantees in life, but a circumstance like Tim's made this truism much more meaningful to me. I savored the time with friends, made even more poignant not knowing what the outcome would be for him, or for that matter, for Stephen. I made a mental note to stay in touch with all four of them when I was back in Michigan.

There'd been no buyers for Meg and Stephen's house, and they talked about taking it off the market until real estate sales improved. They'd stop renting the apartments, because it was a lot of work, and with the possibility of selling the house, it wasn't practical.

I dusted, scrubbed, vacuumed, and mopped, and Gary's house was ready for his return. On May 1, I took a last look around, walked down the stairs, and pulled the big oak door shut. I locked it, pocketed the key, walked through the village, and dropped it *Chez Christine.*

It was a short drive to the village of Gargas, where once again I left my car and suitcases at Mireille and Jean-Claude's. My travel routine kicked in: transported by Mireille to Avignon TGV … teary goodbyes on the platform … train to Charles de Gaulle airport overnight … next-day flight to Traverse City, and … back to Woodmere Cottages.

32 Working on What I Want

THE NEIGHBORS WHO'D TAKEN their condo off the market had listed it for $139,900. Their unit was in a less desirable location than mine, had a different floor plan, and lacked the amenities and upgrades of my unit, which was listed at $147,900. I was momentarily elated when I got a call from an agent in the realtor's office telling me there'd been an offer on my condo! But wait … not so fast. The offer was for $125,000. Talk about low-ball! I found a polite way of saying, "They're nuts!" to the realtor, who suggested we counter. But as we talked about it, I had a feeling this was an omen. Maybe selling the condo wasn't a good idea.

I pushed myself to work in my gardens, which had always been a source of comfort to me. But this summer, even the gardens were being difficult. Plants, which normally bloomed effortlessly, just curled up and sat there, daring me to do something to entice a blossom. The bird feeder hanging in my weeping cherry tree had dropped an infinite number of seeds to the ground over the winter and suddenly, with warm weather, my garden was sprouting sunflowers as well as other strange looking foliage. I pulled out the errant greenery. I wanted blossoms, not unknown vegetation.

The realtor's office was in touch. I decided I would not counter the low-ball offer but agreed to drop my asking price. Maybe the month of July would bring people to town who might be thinking about moving to Traverse City.

My budget looked up when I got an email from a professional photographer who intended to come to Saignon next winter and needed help arranging housing. Gene and his wife had spent time in the village on previous trips and were looking for help setting up another visit when he planned to do some photography workshops. I told him I'd be happy to check for lodging possibilities around the village, and he sent a $50 check to cover my time and efforts.

The off/on/off/on sale couple changed their minds again. Sale on. Then we got a notice from the management company informing us Rod's unit had been sold. I wasn't surprised because at $125,000, it was a steal. He'd sold the condo for less than his dad had paid for it and in so doing had effectively reduced the value of all of the other units. I mentally cursed his son while thinking Rod must be twisting in his grave knowing his offspring had dealt a real blow to those of us who still lived at Woodmere Cottages.

The summer was half over, and there was no condo sale in sight for me. I could no longer stand the uncertainty of not knowing if it would sell in time for me to move to an apartment, so I contacted my realtor. Although my listing contract had a month to run, I told him I was no longer going to sell.

Suddenly I was impatient, and … restless. I'd done pretty well the past few years at not being restless, but there it was again. I needed to get back to France … sooner than later. I was set to go to Michael and Susan's for cat care in October, but I emailed Meg asking her if I could have the apartment starting in September.

July 25, 2012

Meg emailed that I can have the apartment virtually rent-free for September and October (when I won't be at Michael and Susan's) until I move up to Gary's house in the village. Now to settle on a house sitter and Beemer care. Melissa is going to be gone for almost a week in September, and it isn't fair to her for me not to have an alternative for Beemer care to give her a break and also if she wants to travel.

ONCE I'D HEARD FROM MEG, I went online and confirmed my airline ticket. There was a charge for changing the date, but I decided it was a fair price to pay for my sanity and peace of mind.

Having a house sitter would be better than the periodic check in by the handyman or depending on the watchful eyes of the neighbors. The other advantage would be the house sitter would pay the utilities, which, although minimal when the unit was empty, constituted a line item in my budget.

August 1, 2012

The results of my ad for a house sitter on Craig's List are pouring in. I'll set up interviews with those I think might be good candidates.

AN INTERIOR DESIGNER named Gretchen answered my ad. She had her own design business, had just split with a business partner, and was short of money because of the split. She'd been renting near Suttons Bay but wanted to be closer to town. Gretchen was a big woman with long, platinum-blond hair, well made up, and attractively dressed. Large bone-rimmed glasses accented her dark-brown eyes, and she carried herself with confidence. I checked on her references, which were stellar. Added bonus … she was a cat person, so she'd be very happy to take care of Beemer if Melissa needed or wanted to be away. I drew up the house-sitter contract and accepted her security deposit. One month until departure.

In August, Sally left for a week to join her former college chums at their annual reunion. I told Joe I'd come out and spend a few days with him and Will. Gretchen agreed to stay at the condo, which would give her an orientation to the house as well as to Beemer's care.

After a couple of super-nice days with Joe, I went back to Traverse City. I packed boxes to ship to France and cleared the pantry.

I invited Melissa and Gretchen for supper, and they hit it off immediately, for which I was grateful. It was a relief to know my condo and Beemer would be in two pairs of good hands.

Since I'd be in France on Joe's birthday, they invited me to stay with them for the weekend. Gretchen came again to stay with Beemer, and I drove to Empire. Friday evening, we made our way to Frankfort and The Dinghy for fish and chips. It would be a long time before I'd enjoy The Dinghy's fish and chips again. We hung out for the rest of the weekend, and Joe grilled chicken for Sunday lunch. Reluctantly, I said goodbye, promising to stay in touch.

September 3, 2012 Labor Day

Another cool morning. A whirlwind day yesterday, but I'm ready to do the final packing. Melissa dropped by to pick up Beemer. It's time to switch gears. I'll miss Beemer, Joe, and Sally, and my condo, but I'm looking forward to an extended time in France. Meg emailed to ask me what I'd like for supper the night I arrive. She is such a great friend.

33 Back in The Luberon

MIREILLE AND JEAN-CLAUDE met me at the TGV station in Avignon and transported me to my apartment. They'd brought the suitcases and boxes I'd stored with them and helped me haul them in. I thanked them, said good-bye, and unpacked a few basics before heading upstairs for supper with Meg and Stephen. I'd been staying there off and on since 2004. It felt ever so familiar.

"Oh, Meg," I exclaimed, "fish pie. Thank you so much."

"Well, I remembered it was your favorite, and when you said just to fix whatever was easiest, this was as easy as anything."

"Stephen, pour us a glass of wine, will you please?" Meg called out. She was busy in the kitchen, and I noticed the streaks of gray in her brown hair had lightened with the summer sun. Her eyes were snappy and her smile warm as she dried her hands and gave me a hug. Stephen went to work on the drinks and, wine in hand, we sat on the terrace. I gazed around at the familiar sight of walls of stone and sprawling vineyards below the house. I was where I wanted to be; I was in France with dear friends.

As the sun began to sink lower in the sky, we went inside to supper. Shortly after supper, I said goodnight and made my way down the huge slabs of stone stairs to the lower level and my apartment. Tired but happy, I crawled into bed and quickly fell asleep.

The next morning, I was up early feeling surprisingly rested.

Mireille had picked up groceries for me. I had coffee, a baguette, fresh oranges, butter, and marmalade. There was sliced ham for a sandwich at lunch and the ingredients for pasta and salad supper, and, of course, a bottle of local wine. I made coffee, went onto the terrace, and admired the view. The vineyard stretched below with its backdrop of the Luberon hills. Clouds danced on the horizon, and the recently cut fields of lavender formed a patchwork with the vineyards.

I called Gary and arranged to go up to the house in Saignon and retrieve the items I had stashed high up on the shelf of the guest-room closet. We had a nice visit, and I admired the improvements he'd made over the summer. This year, he had installed internet radio in all the rooms. I'd look forward to enjoying it after my November move-in.

I eased back into my Luberon life. The gym, Megaform, put me in the groove of exercise. I often met Meg for coffee at the Aptois Café, our all-time favorite spot. I sat in the café, looked around, and listened to the conversations in French. I felt comfortable … at ease. There was something calming about the custom of sitting over a cup of coffee or a glass of wine, and no one hurries you along. After the chaos and frenetic pace of Traverse City, I was more than ready for a little calm.

One evening, as I sat on the terrace taking in the view and sipping a glass of wine, reality hit me. This was all transient. I'd been coming here since 2004 … eight years. My life had evolved into a daisy chain of transitions and venues. No sooner had I settled into one location, and was enjoying it, then I had to begin thinking about my next move. I was living a series of temporary times.

I'd enjoyed long-term stays since my original adventure caring for the Claparèdes properties. Then there was the six-month stint at Mary and Tim's house while they were in Australia, followed by my year's stay, from 2007 to 2008, in this very apartment. But I couldn't help thinking maybe I should decide on something more permanent.

I'd started with a pattern of two, three, five or six months in France, and the rest of the year at Woodmere Cottages. That pattern had morphed into seven or eight months in France and then Woodmere Cottages. When in France, I'd been cobbling together a couple of months here and a few weeks there at different locations in my desperate attempt to spend more time in my adopted country. When I was in Michigan, I never tried to find ways to stay longer. Instead of feeling settled, I felt as if I were in a holding pattern … waiting to get back to France. My summers in Traverse City were like one big prelude.

When I'd decided to put my condo on the market, I'd had visions of a quick sale, the same as my Glen Arbor experience. My plan had been to sell the condo, downsize to an apartment, which I could sub-let, then find a year-round rental in France. I liked this apartment, but Meg and Stephen might sell the house, so it wasn't an option for a longer stay. I wanted another full year in Provence.

I knew I should have stopped my grousing. Didn't I realize how many people would consider it their dream of a lifetime to be able to enjoy even a small snippet of the experiences I was having? I wasn't ungrateful for the life I was living, or taking it for granted, but I wanted more. Like a chocoholic or an alcoholic, there was never enough. I had to figure out how to expand my time in France. I began to let friends and acquaintances know I was on the lookout for a year-round rental. My very own *pied-à-terre*. I put my desires out there. Who knew what might surface?

34 Another French Connection

IN EARLY OCTOBER, I had an opportunity to have coffee with Jinny, who was Finnish by origin but had been raised in the States. She had moved to France a number of years ago and had an apartment in the center of Apt. It was nice to connect with another American and one who'd settled permanently in France.

Jinny had started a weekly informal conversation group for French speakers wanting to improve their skills in English. It was held Monday evenings at a local education center in Apt. She asked me to go along with her to meet the group and see if I'd be interested in filling in as leader, when she might be traveling.

October 9, 2012

Late yesterday, I went into town and met Jinny and stayed for the English language group. It was VERY satisfying and interesting. I will happily fill in for her when she's not around. It makes me feel more connected to the French community.

IN THE MIDDLE OF THE MONTH, I moved to Michael and Susan's. I arrived a day before they were to leave for Italy, and we spent time with final house and cat orientation. Both animals were

senior citizens, and one required a daily pill, but it was nothing I hadn't done before.

The house was enormous, set in an expanse of fields surrounded by hills. Originally a farmhouse with attached barn, the entire building was beautifully restored and converted into a magnificent home. I'd be staying in an apartment that was at the back of the house on the upper level, and could be accessed either from within the house via a stairway or by its own outside entrance. I'd have my own private space with easy access to downstairs, where the cats were fed and had their litter boxes.

October 16, 2012

The sun is streaming in the windows of this apartment. Pussycat is curled up on my fleece jacket, in a sunny spot. I moved in late Sunday. We had champagne and a nice supper. Yesterday morning I drove them into Apt to get the bus. By afternoon I was ready to sit in the sun and read.

THE CATS WERE EASY AND AFFECTIONATE. Orlando was old, skinny, sweet, and very arthritic. He was a mottled tan and white color and loved to sleep on the bed. Pussycat was a round, loveable fluff of black and white. I had my challenges getting her daily pill down her, but we succeeded.

One evening, as I sat curled up on the sofa, the two cats at my feet, I looked around the room. I could live here, I thought to myself, and began to imagine myself permanently installed in the warm and comfortable apartment. There it was, the "never enough" syndrome. I sighed and went back to my book.

The evening of their return, Michael and Susan took a taxi from the bus station in Apt and, once they'd settled in, I invited them for a light supper of tomato cheese tart, salad, and a recounting of the sights they'd seen in Italy. The next morning, showered with their thanks and even more money than I'd expected, I said goodbye and returned to my apartment chez Meg and Stephen.

I'd done research on housing in and around Saignon for the photographer, Gene, and after a lot of back-and-forth emails with Lizzie, she offered him the Lantins for a modest rent plus utilities. I connected the two of them via email and bowed out of the process. I'd work with Gene once he had dates for his arrival in France. Even as I researched housing for Gene, my own search for more permanent lodging was never far from my mind. I took notes. One never knew when something perfect would appear.

Early in November, I went up to Gary's house, and we did a walk through so I could see the changes he'd made. I got a refresher course on the heating system and some of the new controls he'd installed on various electronic devices. True to form, Gary never left anything simple.

I'd just gotten back to the apartment when Meg came by in a panic. They'd received a card in the mail from the water company saying their meter was showing excessively high readings, which could only mean there was a leak somewhere. Water was expensive enough, and a leak could mean a financial blow!

November 10, 2012

Meg came down yesterday wildly trying to find someone who could come and locate the water leak. Sophie, the cleaning lady, was there, and she called a plumber friend of hers who came immediately and located the leak, just outside the house where the water comes in. It was an eye-opening episode. Stephen just does not function well in an emergency. He is not physically strong, and I watched him really struggle to lift the heavy metal manhole cover over the spot where the water meter dials are located. Later, while Meg was frantically trying to find a solution, he sat quietly on the sofa playing solitaire on the computer. It was also a bit disarming to see Meg in such a state. She was near tears, clearly very shaken, and concerned about the cost.

CATHY HAD COME TO JOIN GARY for a short time, so I went to the village for a visit. She was tall and slender, had auburn hair, and spoke with a British-accented soft voice. It was nice to be able to connect with both of them. After all, it was her house as well as his, although I most often thought of it as "Gary's house." We had a nice visit, and it felt good to get better acquainted.

I spent a couple more weeks in the apartment and then moved to their house. It was a quick two-day move in and out, because I was due at Paul and Anne's for a week of cat sitting. I unpacked the essentials and gathered what I needed to take to Roussillon.

Here I was hooking together weeks at different venues like railroad cars on a train. I'd been in Meg and Stephen's apartment, then at Michael and Susan's, back to the apartment, moved up to Gary's just long enough to deposit my belongings, and then off I went to Paul and Anne's. Nice people, nice places, and the cat-sitting helped pay the bills. It wasn't as if I had to move all of my things, but I had to admit that what had been exciting and challenging was beginning to be tiring. What had changed? Had I?

I enjoyed being at Paul and Anne's. Sebby immediately became my bed buddy and, fluffy, furry Ellie found her spot on my bedroom chair. Frankie was up to her usual appearance at meal times but otherwise out and about. There were often times when she appeared that I had visions of Sheba and Freddy. The Provençal sun had taken its toll on Sebby's ears and nose with some nasty looking sores and growths, but he did not appear to be in pain, and the vet had said there was really nothing to do for the time being.

35 Another American Visitor

PHOTOGRAPHER GENE WAS DUE to arrive a few days before Thanksgiving. Joelle was helping Lizzie, who was in Australia, and would let him in and do the orientation to the Lantins. There were meters to be read to gauge the amount of fuel and electricity he'd use. Lizzie and family would be coming at Christmas, during which time Gene would go back to the States. Utilities were very expensive in France, and Gene was to pay only for what he consumed. The meters would be read, and Lizzie would pay for the time she and her family were in residence.

I drove to Saignon to meet him and liked him immediately. Gene was short with a full head of curly, snow-white hair. He moved quickly and purposefully, and I put him somewhere in his fifties. He had bright blue eyes and an easy smile.

For a change on Thanksgiving Day, I had no plans, which felt surprisingly good. It wasn't a holiday in France, and I'd grown tired of trying to re-create one. In spite of the efforts of Meg and others, it was just not the same. The day before, I received an email from Gene saying he'd come down with a cold. I told him to meet me the next day at the pharmacy in Apt, and I'd help him get some cold remedies. He agreed and suggested we go out for lunch afterwards.

We had a pleasant lunch at a restaurant in Apt. It was a different Thanksgiving, but very enjoyable. He was open, friendly, and in spite of his head cold, was cheerful and eager to find out all he could about Apt and the area. Gene was an extraordinarily talented photographer, and almost immediately began sending photos via email. The buildings and vistas that I'd been looking at on a regular basis I saw anew through the lens of his camera. The images were superb!

At the end of a week, Paul and Anne returned. I went back to Saignon and got seriously busy settling into the house for the winter. It felt good to put my bathroom articles away, organize my clothes in the closet, and make my nest.

Meg called and said she and Stephen wanted to take me out to dinner for my birthday, and she suggested *La Petite Cave* restaurant just down the quay. This would be a very nice birthday treat, because a meal at *La Petite Cave* was excellent cuisine, and also not in my budget.

December 1, 2012

I had a really nice birthday. Meg called in the morning, and I picked up some croissants and went down for tea. Later, Gene came up to bring me a bottle of champagne and wished me a happy birthday. We had a nice meal at the Petite Cave, and the chef came out and talked to us. I have such happy memories of my birthdays in France.

ONE OF THE WOMEN in Jinny's Monday-evening English-conversation group lived just outside of Saignon and offered to give me a ride. Her offer saved me from driving after dark and from losing my parking place on the quay, plus I really appreciated this additional connection to the French community. The more French people I knew, the more I felt as if I belonged.

I'd moved into the village house, resumed my Luberon activities, and pretended I lived in France. The pattern of winters in Gary and Cathy's village house looked promising as an ongoing arrangement. I had at least six months before I needed to think about packing up and moving. I'd be going to stay at Paul and Anne's for several weeks, but my base was the Saignon house. I was feeling pretty smug about *ma vie en France*.

As Christmas approached, I was caught in my usual dilemma of not wanting to enter into the never-ending round of parties. Gene left for Christmas in the States. Meg called and said Stephen was not feeling well. His health had been an ongoing issue, but some of his symptoms had gotten to the point where his doctor had advised him to go to the Apt hospital for extensive testing. I offered to let Miel out for a walk and feed her.

The schedule for Stephen's medical testing didn't allow for holiday parties, so Meg canceled their traditional pre-Christmas mulled-wine and mince-pie gathering. His test results showed a possible growth on the liver, and doctors had diagnosed hemochromatosis, a blood disorder causing his blood to produce too much iron. Old fashioned as it sounded, the treatment was periodic bleeding, for which he had to make trips to the hospital. Holiday festivities took a back seat. I was concerned about Stephen but turned my attention to my upcoming stay with the cats in Roussillon. I packed up what I'd need and made the move.

I had invited Nicole and Brigitte for Christmas lunch with me at Paul and Anne's. I roasted a turkey with stuffing and candied some sweet potatoes. This was my fifth Christmas at Paul and Anne's house. It felt familiar to me now, and I pretended it was my house or, as the French say I was, *chez moi.*

December 28, 2012

Yesterday I went over to Saignon and walked Miel in the morning and in the afternoon and fed her. Meg called from the hospital and later after they got home. The most recent scan didn't show the growth on Stephen's liver, which is odd, but he does have liver damage and needs an MRI.

ON DECEMBER 28, I left my furry friends in Roussillon and returned to the village house in Saignon. I had effectively dodged invitations for New Year's Eve celebrations and instead had a quiet evening on my own.

The holidays, Stephen's health, moving from Roussillon back to Saignon, all coalesced to make me feel tired and depressed. Much as I loved Gary's house (Gary and Cathy's house), it took a lot of effort to keep clean, which wasn't easy.

I organized tax numbers for the accountant in Traverse City and juggled my finances. I didn't do much driving here in France and the Old Gray Mare was good on gas mileage, but with the price of gas and the exchange rate, a fill up was the equivalent of $90. The more I crunched the numbers, the more I knew I was walking a financial tightrope. So far, I'd kept my balance.

January 19, 2013

There's a cold rain, almost snow. Yesterday was cold and windy, but I had a great day. I vacuumed and mopped floors, did laundry and fixed a meat loaf supper for Meg, Stephen and Gene. The evening was a huge success. Meat loaf is Stephen's favorite and nice to have another American to enjoy it. Gene is coming for a French lesson, and I need to start putting things together for next week when I move to Paul and Anne's.

36 Frustration

ON JANUARY 22, I LOCKED UP the house on rue Cilly and moved back to Roussillon. I was looking forward to a peaceful month of cat companionship. Then the Electric Company (EDF) mailed a notice saying the electricity would be off most of one day during the week. The alarm company called, because one of the rental houses Paul and Anne took care of had problems with the alarm system. A stray cat began wandering around and even came in the cat flap one day. So much for peace and quiet.

Gene came for a French lesson, and I invited him to stay for lunch. He was a positive person; his presence was a boost to my morale and his payment for lessons a boost to my bottom line. I had to hand it to him; he was getting around, meeting people and making the most of his time and photo ops. He was creating a photographic book of Provence—his take on the people and places.

My Woodmere condo and Traverse City were never completely off my radar. Gretchen emailed to let me know the hot water heater was acting up. I'd left her with the necessary phone numbers for maintenance and repairs and told her to go ahead and call the plumbing and heating company. It wasn't the first time the hot water heater had been an issue, so I was annoyed but not surprised.

In February, all hell broke loose between Gene and Lizzie. When Gene had gone back to the States at Christmas, Lizzie and family stayed at the Lantins. The meters were to be read when Lizzie arrived, and once more when she and the family departed. Somewhere between the agreement and the actual activity, there was a breakdown, and Lizzie was suddenly demanding large sums of money from Gene, in addition to what he'd already paid her up front. I'd had my experiences with Lizzie's record keeping as well as her not keeping her word, so I wasn't surprised when the situation arose with Gene. She claimed she'd forgotten to read the meters and was basing her figures on estimates.

March 6, 2013

Spent time yesterday helping Gene draft a letter to Lizzie, replies and copies this morning. What a mess! Now she's asking Gene to leave the property.

AFTER A DAY OR SO, I realized something had to be done about Gene's situation, so I called Meg and asked if they'd be willing to rent the apartment to him for the remaining week of his stay. They agreed, and he was grateful for my help.

Gene spent his remaining days taking photos. As his departure date grew close, I helped him arrange his train to Paris, the overnight hotel at the airport, and a flight back to the States. All in all, he'd had a great stay in Saignon. It was too bad the experience ended on a sour note. Unfortunately, he'd paid Lizzie a lot of money up front and had evidence via email communications that she'd been at best unreasonable and at worst, dishonest. In the end he opted not to go to the hassle of getting a lawyer and trying to recoup his expenses. He was a good sport about it, and philosophically chalked it up to the price he'd paid to learn a lesson about giving someone money upfront.

March 12, 2013

I saw Joelle in town, and we had a good talk about Lizzie's behavior. It seems this is not the first time Lizzie has (conveniently) "forgotten" to follow up on reading meters for renter's costs.

IN THE MIDST OF THE LIZZIE VS. GENE FIASCO, I had to get to Avignon to file for my *Carte* renewal. Once it was done, I relaxed a little. A few days later, I got confirmation from Gary that I could rent the house for the coming winter of 2013-2014. I also got confirmation from the Préfecture in Avignon they would hold my *Carte* for me to pick up when I returned in the fall.

March 31, 2013 Easter Sunday

The rain and fog are gone, and there's a fierce Mistral in their place. Mireille called and invited me to lunch tomorrow. I've really pared down my belongings. Got an email from Joe and Sally. They are vacationing in Florida. One more month here in Saignon and then back to Michigan.

I HAD BEEN PREPARED to have Gretchen as a housemate, just as I had done with Melissa, but she emailed to say she would be spending the summer with a friend. I'd have the condo completely to myself, and she'd come back when I returned to France. Anticipating another Michigan summer, I turned my energy to packing.

Gary and Cathy had several nicely painted wicker baskets where they stashed things when vacating. The baskets were attractive, there was space in the guest bedroom to put a couple of them, and Gary was agreeable for me to leave a few things stored there. Nicole and I took a trip to Avignon so I could buy baskets for myself. I wouldn't have to pack up everything … and it would be a good feeling to know my things were in place for my return.

The day before departure, I took my car to Mireille and Jean-Claude's, and they drove me back to Saignon. Gary was due to arrive in the evening. The next day, he took me to Avignon and the TGV, and I was off to Michigan. It had been such an enjoyable winter and early spring in the Luberon. I tried to muster my enthusiasm for my return to the States but really didn't have much luck.

37 An Unlucky Number

BACK STATESIDE, THE CULTURAL DIFFERENCES struck me harder than past years. The bigger, better, supersized atmosphere made me uncomfortable, and I struggled to re-establish my nest in the condo. Gretchen had done a good job of looking after things, but she was clearly not big on housekeeping. One look in the refrigerator, and I knew I'd have to scrub it down before adding any food.

She'd managed to muddle up the built-in speaker system I used to listen to FM radio and sometimes play the TV audio. I tried to fix it myself, but I finally had to have a repairman come in. He quickly corrected the problem, which was just a matter of her having plugged cords into the wrong input and my having pushed a wrong button in my attempts to solve the issue. A thirty-five-dollar lesson in electronics. None of this was earth shattering, life threatening, or even a big expense, but it was irritating.

It didn't help my morale to get an email from Gary with a not-so-subtle complaint about things I'd stored. In addition to the baskets he'd okay'd, I'd shoved a plastic bag of winter sweaters under the bed and stashed two plastic boxes of toiletries on a shelf in the closet, which required standing on a small ladder to reach. Gary saw fit to make a comment that we'd have to "talk about storage," since, as "you well know," there was "so little space" available. I don't think it was about storage. I think it was more about being possessive of his property and not wanting any evidence someone else lived there. How easy it was for him to ignore the fact I'd been giving ownership care to his house and car. His comments reminded me of how unappreciated I'd felt by Lizzie and Andrew, and of how much I didn't like that feeling.

With Joe and Sally working, I waited until the weekend to visit. I took my usual stash of "goodies from France," but once they were delivered, I had the feeling the novelty had worn off. We caught up on news, and Joe grilled steaks for supper. I appreciated the tasty steak, since I'd never been able to find beef in France with any flavor and had finally given up trying. There was something really satisfying about a good, old, American rib eye.

I made my rounds of medical appointments and resumed work with a trainer at the gym, all of which made me increasingly aware of my age and the fact that time was creeping up on me. I was in good health, but who knew how long I could count on that? The eye doctor told me I had cataracts. Don't *old* people get those? It was a tiny wake-up call and made me even more determined to find a way to spend another year in Provence. I was tired of cobbling weeks and months together so I could be there and not here. I'd talked to Meg about possibly renting the apartment in the fall, which would allow me to go to France before Gary vacated the Saignon house. She and Stephen had agreed, which meant I could leave Michigan in September. Maybe I could ask them about another extended rental period when I left Gary's house the following spring. Maybe.

Then, somewhat fortuitously, Gretchen stopped by to pick up a few things she'd stored in the basement.

"Hi Jo Anne, are you getting settled in?"

"Pretty much so, although it has been a bit challenging. How about you?" I asked. (I decided not to comment on her housekeeping skills and screwed-up stereo system. It would serve no purpose.)

"Oh, it's okay," she replied. "My friend's house has a completely separate apartment downstairs, so I have plenty of space, and we share meals, and I help her take care of things."

We chatted for a while about her interior design business, which happily for her was picking up. Staying in my condo had helped her bottom line, and now she was getting more and more clients.

"I was wondering," she said, "If I paid you more money than utilities, would you be able to stay on in France next summer?"

I listened without responding immediately, but my mind kicked into gear. "Maybe," I finally replied. "I could see if Meg and Stephen would be open to my renting again for a longer period of time."

We agreed that I would check on my housing options in France for next summer and beyond. I also knew it would be a big help to Gretchen if she didn't have to move out of the condo the following spring.

May 29, 2013

I finally got an email from Meg with an OK for the apartment this fall. She also expressed concerns about Stephen's health.

WITH THE POSSIBILITY OF ANOTHER yearlong stay in France, I got proactive. I took masses of papers to be shredded and donated odds and ends to a northern Michigan charity, The Father Fred Foundation. I looked through my art supplies and culled out paper and paints, which I donated to an educational nonprofit, Blackbird Arts, just down the street. I had supplies in France, where I painted now, and I hadn't done any watercolors in Michigan for several years. Why hang on to supplies? If an extended absence from here became a reality, I'd be ready.

The weather finally turned summery, and I bought more annuals and hanging baskets. If I had to be here, I was going to make my outdoor surroundings as pleasant and colorful as possible. But, just as I had my world beautified with flowers, Michigan weather reared its ugly head and frost warnings meant I had to drag everything inside or at least under cover for several nights. Another reminder of the contrasts in weather between northern Michigan and southern France.

Then I got an email from Michael and Susan asking me to do some house- and cat-sitting for them in October. I had really enjoyed staying in their apartment, and this would help my finances.

Periodically, I got email messages from Meg. She was a two-fingered typist; hers and Stephen's social calendar was always brimming, so I knew it wasn't easy for her to communicate either in detail or with regularity. When she did write, she'd express increasing concern about Stephen's health. He was being treated for the hemochromatosis and also for a heart problem. The conditions were under control, but worrying.

In July, I decided to have my cataracts taken care of. Although the doctor had said I could wait, I wasn't big on waiting for anything and, in the back of my mind I was thinking I might be gone to France for a whole year. If that was going to be the case, it felt better to take care of medical things sooner rather than later. The surgeries went well, but I ended up being nearsighted, a condition quickly remedied with glasses. I was told that once the eyes had completely healed, I could wear contact lenses. I'd worn contacts for years so wasn't at all upset by the prospect, and at least I wouldn't have to worry about cataract surgery when I got to the Luberon.

On July 27, I woke to an email from Meg saying Stephen was in the hospital and it didn't look good. I sat there looking at the screen and wondering what had happened. I decided to call her later, but before I could follow up, I got another email message from Meg:

"Stephen died this morning."

I was stunned.

July 28, 2013

It's raining and very cool! A few emails from Meg. Stephen's son-in-law, Roger, is on his way, driving from Germany where he's living and working. His wife, Maria, flying in today from the States. This is surreal. I cannot believe Stephen is gone!

DURING THE FOLLOWING DAYS, there were more email messages regarding plans for Stephen's funeral. He would be cremated in France, and his ashes would remain there. I just could not bring myself to believe it. Sure, he had health issues, but nothing indicated he was near death.

I was unnerved by Stephen's passing. I continued to think about him, his life, and France. It made me think more realistically about my own age and life and what I really wanted to do ... where I really wanted to be. It wasn't as if I was in my twenties, or even thirties, with lots of time ahead of me. I was 77 years old!

August 24, 2013

Feeling a bit "out of sorts." The reality of life settling in. Called Meg yesterday and had a nice long talk. She sounds awful. Melissa picked me up and we went for pizza and salad, then out to Glen Arbor for a gallery show opening by a friend of hers. I had feelings of déjà vu ... all the Friday-night openings during the years I'd lived there. Also, a painful reminder of how many of my artist friends have died ... my painting teacher and mentor, Suzanne, the couple who started the gallery years ago, and neighbor Rod, who always showed up for the openings. And now the latest, Stephen in France. Time to stop and smell the roses and be where I really want to be .... in France.

I MADE THE MOST of my remaining weeks in Traverse City. I prepped the condo in anticipation of Gretchen's return for the winter. I mailed boxes to France and reserved my train ticket from Paris to Avignon. I alerted Mireille to my arrival, and she assured me she and Jean-Claude would meet me. Meg emailed she'd have a *kir* and supper waiting for my arrival. A *kir*! I could almost taste the delightful mix of chilled white wine with black currant liqueur. If I were lucky, it would be a *kir royale*, made with champagne.

My positive attitude was beginning to return. I was good to go.

September 2, 2013 Labor Day

Light rain and significantly cooler .... Autumn on the way, and so am I. I took Beemer to Melissa's yesterday afternoon and he settled right in, which made it much easier to leave him. I drove out to Joe and Sally's to celebrate his birthday. We took a walk, and Joe grilled pork chops, which we ate along with fresh corn and salad.

38 Complications

A BLUR AND THE BLINK OF AN EYE, or so it felt to me, and I was back in France. Mireille and Jean Claude met me at the train and transported me to Saignon, where Meg was waiting with *kir* and supper as promised. Stephen wasn't there to give me his usual bear hug, and Meg and I had a good cry before we ate our meal. The setting was familiar, but it didn't feel the same.

Stephen's absence was a cloud hanging over us. I thought back to the times when his behavior had puzzled me … the day he became belligerent because I'd forgotten to order a book for him. He'd had a mercurial personality. He was capable of sudden outbursts of anger but could turn around and be caring, helping me with the apartment fireplace, and fixing pasta Alfredo for my birthday supper. His behavior had been an enigma, but he was a good man at heart, he'd died too soon, and I missed him.

Meg was doing pretty well, but how can anyone adjust to the sudden and unexpected death of a spouse? Oh, sure, she'd complained about Stephen's reluctance to do any work around the house and the amount of time he spent playing bridge on the computer. What wife didn't find reason to complain about her husband's actions or inactions? She'd loved him and was grief stricken. I helped around the grounds with raking leaves, pruning shrubs, and listening, when she felt the need to talk.

As the days wore on, Meg learned Stephen had died without a will or having his business and personal affairs in order. According to French law, a house does not automatically pass to the surviving spouse, unless special legal papers have been filed. Those had not been filed, and Meg's house now belonged one-half to her and one-half to Stephen's two grown daughters from his first marriage. Fortunately, Meg had an excellent relationship with the daughters, who did their best to make the situation as easy as possible for her. But she'd always deferred to Stephen in financial matters, so had no idea where she stood in terms of resources, and it would take months to sort out. Talk about a blow!

In October, I moved over to care for Orlando and Pussycat while Michael and Susan took a ten-day trip to Italy.

October 14, 2013

Settled in with the cats. I've organized their special spots with Orlando's bed on the easy chair and my old fleece on the sofa for Pussycat. Orlando was settled next to me last night on the sofa, and one of his claws got caught in my sweater. When I went to help pull it free, he nipped the back of my right hand. Poor guy, I know he's so arthritic, and I must have hurt him. I washed my hand with soap and water.

WHEN I WOKE UP the next morning, my right hand was inflamed and swollen. So, I started the day by going to the Centre Médical to get an antibiotic for the cat bite. Then, walking back from the pharmacy, I tripped on the curb, fell, and slammed the sore hand down on the sidewalk. I felt I'd misjudged the distance with my post-cataract surgery eyesight.

When I called Meg and told her my hand was swollen and painful, she insisted on taking me to the hospital emergency room in Apt. My hand and wrist were examined, x-rays taken, and medication given for pain. Luckily, it appeared nothing was broken.

The following days were tough. My right hand was sore, almost useless, and the infection persisted. Meg and my American friend, Laurie, shopped for me and brought food. I had some rudimentary use of the hand, but taking care of the cats and myself was a challenge. I was adamant no one tell Michael and Susan. They were well into their Italy trip, and there was no way I wanted them to turn around and come back because of my clumsiness.

Driving the car was out of the question; shifting gears was impossible. I managed repeated trips to doctors and the hospital with Meg, Laurie, and Anne transporting me. I had a lot of arthritis in the hand (as was so graciously pointed out to me by the doctor going over the x-ray). This did not help the healing or my morale.

Cataracts! Arthritis! *Old* people have those maladies!

Okay, so I was a senior citizen, but I had no intention of crawling off to a retirement home. I was in France and I had things I wanted to do. Bit by bit, the infection cleared and I gradually regained most of the use of my hand.

I felt absolutely no malice toward poor Orlando. He'd reacted to pain. He had only nicked the surface of the skin but, there's nothing worse than the bacteria residing in a cat's mouth, and it takes only a drop of saliva to cause infection. I was lucky it hadn't been more serious.

Michael and Susan returned from their trip and were appalled I had stayed on in spite of the injury; but they were also extremely grateful. Meg helped me move back into the apartment and kept me under her wing. Gary had returned to New York for the winter, and friends in the village were checking on the house until I could move in.

November 17, 2013

I feel as if I'm crawling out of a big, black hole. Five weeks of infection and a sprained wrist. I finally got the all clear from the doctor. The infection is gone and I can (when I want) drive, use my hand "normally". Now it remains for me to regain my confidence and be ready to shift my emotional gears. I'm not going to be in a hurry to move up to Gary's house in Saignon, but plan to stay here at Meg's. Maybe until Christmas.

MEG INVITED SEVERAL COUPLES for a Thanksgiving meal, and I joined them. It was a pleasant afternoon, although we were all well aware this was our first American holiday without Stephen.

The weekend after Thanksgiving, Meg drove above Saignon, and we took Miel for a walk around the Claparèdes lavender fields. As we walked the path around the fields, I was reminded of the beauty of the plant. Even in winter, long after the harvest in June and July, the plant showed a faint-purple hue. The harvesting machines left the rows symmetrically shorn, cylindrical in shape. There was no aroma now, but it didn't take much to conjure up that soothing scent of lavender in full bloom and the accompanying buzzing of hundreds of bees as they collected pollen. In recent years, lavender oil had increased in popularity. The aroma's ability to enhance relaxation meant widespread use in spas ... and lavender-scented soaps also gained a reputation for their calming properties. Occasionally, we'd spot an errant plant with winter blossoms. I plucked a few and took them. The fragrance was delightful. Oh, how I loved being in lavender land!

Finishing our walk, we headed to the car. With Meg along, I screwed up my courage and drove the car back, driving for the first time since I'd fallen. My hand felt just fine manipulating the gearshift, but in spite of my physical healing, I dragged my feet over moving to the village.

It had been a long time since my self-confidence had been as severely shaken as it had been by the cat bite and my subsequent sidewalk tumble. It was going to take even more time to regain it completely. I enjoyed being close to Meg and Miel. I was reassured knowing someone was near should I need help, and I sensed my presence was helpful to Meg. It was easier for her to be away for extended periods of time, because I was there to look after Miel, and she appreciated my assistance with yard work. It also was nice for us both to have a friend to share a drink, a meal—our feelings.

I decided I'd stay in the apartment at least until the end of the month, my birthday. On that day, Meg fixed a lovely supper. The menu was my favorite: fish pie, with a salad and a lovely bottle of wine. It suited us both to celebrate quietly.

December 2, 2013

Bit by bit will start moving things up to the house in Saignon. BIG news that Melissa's friend, Sue, may be interested in buying my condo. I've sent pictures. Who knows? Am feeling a little better about leaving here. My hand is steadily improving. Need to get through December and on to a new year.

MEG WAS IN THE THROES of resolving her financial affairs and talked of selling the house. I hadn't realized how comfortable I had been, knowing the apartment was there as an option for my lodging. If the house sold, I'd have to search elsewhere. If Melissa's friend bought my condo, I could stay on in France for another "year in Provence," but now … there was more uncertainty about where I might stay for such an extended period of time.

Paul and Anne had asked me to do my usual Christmas gig with the cats and to come again in January for six weeks while they traveled to South Africa, and I'd accepted. Suddenly, however, Paul had some health challenges, and their plans were in limbo. He'd not been feeling well and had gone to the hospital for tests. More health issues for my friends, and more housing uncertainty for me.

I paid Gary my December rent and took things up to the Saignon house. Meg said it was no problem for me to leave some belongings in the apartment, which was a relief. I was living with one foot there and the other in the village. Not a particularly comfortable position, but I was procrastinating about the move. Part of me wanted the lightness and brightness of the Saignon house, but in spite of the comparable darkness in the apartment, I was comfortable, felt secure and yes, needed, as I helped Meg with Miel and tasks. There I was again with my age-old nemesis of wanting to be in two places at once. At least these two didn't have an ocean separating them.

39 Places and Possibilities

ANNE EMAILED saying Paul had been diagnosed with diabetes and was starting on insulin, so both their Christmas and South Africa trips were in limbo. I felt bad for them, and for me. I hated uncertainty, and now I was awash in it.

The second week of December, I gathered my confidence and determination, said goodbye to Meg, loaded stuff in the car, and made the move up to Gary's house. I let out a loud sigh of relief when I managed to snag my favorite parking space just below the house. Unpacked and organized, I looked around—I was moved in and on my own.

Gary's heating system did not permit a rapid increase in temperature, so he had purchased a propane gas burner for a quick boost on chilly mornings. The tank was in an unattractive, dark green, square metal box with a small window where the flame was visible when lit, and he'd stashed the contraption inside the fireplace. There was no way I was going to use that ugly monster! It was late in the season to order firewood. I'd been so undecided about when or if I'd be there for winter, I hadn't done it earlier. I made a call, and luckily my usual man had wood left, which he delivered and stacked for me.

The following week, I went to Meg's for a vineyard walk with her and Miel, and learned there was a new development. A couple living in the nearby hamlet had friends from Germany who had expressed an interest in buying her house and wanted to come for a visit. Stephen's daughters were open to her selling the house, but how much she would get for it and how much she'd have after she divided the proceeds with them was unknown.

In light of Stephen's death, Meg was not up to hosting her annual Christmas drinks party; however, there were the usual ex-pat rounds of drinks and dinners. I managed to dodge invitations and enjoyed the peace, quiet, and TV in front of the fireplace. A real fire, not a gas burner.

I DIDN'T KNOW IT AT THE TIME, but the Universe was planting seeds during that Christmas holiday, which would grow and impact my life in the coming year.

Over the years, Joe and Sally had often gone to the Florida Keys for Christmas. This year, however, they'd decided to check out a place called "The Villages" just north of Orlando in Central Florida. The Villages was a planned retirement community with dozens of golf courses and a myriad of organized sports, clubs, and activities, where the main mode of transportation was a golf cart. Joe and Sally were checking it out as a possible destination for their retirement. In spite of a snowstorm, they'd managed to get out of Michigan, and on Christmas Eve, I got an email that they'd arrived safely. I was happy to hear it, but I couldn't help but wonder: What would it mean if they moved to Florida?

I got an email saying Melissa's friend, Sue, wanted to visit the condo, so I contacted Gretchen to arrange the visit. After her visit, Sue indicated an interest in buying, but she already owned a house near downtown Traverse City, so she wasn't in a position to do anything immediately. Retirement in Florida and a possible buyer for my condo were like packages under the Christmas tree that I couldn't unwrap until later.

With Paul's diabetes under control, he and Anne left Christmas Eve for a family holiday in England, and I moved in with the cats. Brigitte had invited me to join her, Nicole, Brigitte's daughter, and

her daughter's boyfriend for Christmas lunch. It was ten minutes up the road in the village of Goult, where I'd stayed in the studio apartment, and I was happy to be included.

We had a lovely lunch with oysters, salmon, chicken with veggies, the traditional French cheese tray, salad, and a lovely *bûche de Noël* I'd picked up from Mireille. It was a nice, quiet family celebration of the holiday. I thanked Brigitte for a lovely day and was back in Roussillon with the cats well before dark.

The remainder of the holiday week I enjoyed the sunny terrace and company of my feline buddies. I spent New Year's Eve my favorite way … in front of the fireplace with TV and Sebby curled up next to me. I watched as 2014 was welcomed in around the world, and then went to bed wondering what the coming year held in store for me. I surely hoped it would not be as unlucky as 2013.

New Year's Day, 2014

A few high clouds overhead, but mostly sunny. I went to the bakery in the village and got a baguette to leave for Paul and Anne and one for me. I made a big pot of chili and will leave some and take some back with me. Melissa's friend, Sue, emailed that she's set to offer to buy my condo, when she sells her house and I've sent her my asking price.

I GATHERED MY THINGS and returned to Saignon. The weather was gray and rainy. When the rain stopped, the Mistral started howling. I didn't know which was worse. I tried to feel optimistic about the New Year, but I felt as unsettled as the weather.

I struggled with my vision. My eyes had not been quite right since last summer's cataract surgeries, and I felt my eyesight had contributed to my falling on the sidewalk in October. I went to a local optometrist who did a vision test and ordered contact lenses for me to try. Fingers crossed.

I had hoped to be able to stay in Meg's apartment when Gary returned to the Saignon house in the spring, but if Meg sold the house I would not have that option. Now what would I do?

One afternoon, a census taker came knocking at the door with a form she needed to complete and have signed by Gary. She asked me a few questions about who lived in the house and for how many months. I gave her as little information as possible, but she had her mind made up according to the directions she'd been given, and continued checking boxes about whether this was a primary or secondary residence. When I scanned and emailed the form to Gary, he had a fit. We finally sorted it all out, but not before I was made to feel as if I'd done something terrible. No matter what I did, or how much care I gave the house, I often felt I could not win with Gary. I renewed my resolve to find a solution to my long-term housing in France.

On February 3, Paul and Anne left for an extended vacation in South Africa. I was pleased for them that Paul was dealing with his diabetes, and I moved over to Roussillon happy to have an entire month taking care of the house and the cats. I was also grateful for Gary's offer of free rent in return for periodic Saignon trips to check the heating-system pressure gauges, plug in the battery charger on the car, collect any mail from the box, flush the toilets, run the faucets, and adjust the timers on various lights and lamps set to ensure a lived-in look.

With housing options unsettled, it felt good to again relax on the sunny terrace and enjoy the company of Ellie, Frankie, and my bed buddy, Sebby.

A few days after I arrived, Sue emailed agreeing to my asking price on the condo. We could move ahead and sign a purchase agreement with the contingency that she must first sell her house. I knew this process was going to be tricky—we were on opposite sides of the ocean—but I took comfort in knowing she was a friend of Melissa's. Scanned and emailed signatures were legally binding, so how hard could it be? At long last, I could rid myself of the financial and emotional responsibilities of owning a house.

It turned out my confidence in the ease of handling the sale was misplaced. Sue might have been a friend of Melissa's, but she did not demonstrate any of Melissa's more positive personality traits. She immediately assumed an "I'm in charge" attitude and began making demands about how the procedure would unfold. In desperation, I contacted my financial adviser, Pete, whom I also counted as a friend, and asked him if I could pay him to handle this process. I was willing to give him Power of Attorney (POA) for the sale of the house, which turned out to be a great idea but an almost impossible task to accomplish.

In order for me to give Pete the POA, I had to sign a form and have my signature notarized. I took the form to the Marie, but the secretary in the mayor's office refused to notarize it because the document was not in French. I then learned translating legal documents into French had to be done by a very limited (and very expensive) number of individuals. Why did everything have to be so complicated?

After more days of frustrating interchanges with Sue, I basically backed off before I said or did something I might regret. The woman was totally unreasonable. Pete met with her and confirmed my impressions. She was demanding, acting as if this sale involved only her and would be done her way.

I tried not to worry too much about the future. Some days it was easier than others. I couldn't help thinking of how easy it could be to spend time in France if I no longer owned the condo. But ... I needed to be patient, and that never had been easy for me. I did my best to just enjoy being with the cats in Roussillon. Condo sale be damned.

40 Transitions

IT HAD BEEN TEN YEARS since I'd arrived all full of enthusiasm to take over as guardian of the Domaine des Claparèdes. Ten years of ping pong over the ocean. Ten years of cobbling together venues so I could spend more time in France. I longed for some resolution to the uncertainty. To be settled once and for all in lavender land.

Emails from Pete and Sue back in Michigan were not reassuring, but I tamped down my irritation. Pete was handling Sue, who was turning out to be a real piece of work. I took the long view. I'd deal with her antics, if it meant selling the condo so I'd be free to spend as much time as I wanted in France.

Meg's house sale to the German couple was all but finalized. She went to the *notaire's* office to sign the purchase agreement, when suddenly the prospective buyers decided they wanted to add another contingency and refused to sign. This meant she would be in limbo for another three months, while more paperwork was filed at the Mairie and processed.

Assuming the condo sale would go through, I was going to need a place to live once I returned to Michigan. When I'd had the condo on the market previously, I'd looked at apartments in Traverse City, and contacted one complex about availability. The rental agent said she'd send me the paperwork to be added to their waiting list since they were full.

Gary was to arrive mid-April. With the hiatus in Meg's house sale, I might be able to move into her apartment when I left Gary's house, but no firm dates were set. My options were dangling.

Meg was not completely comfortable with the prospect of my moving back into the apartment. She expressed concern "someone" might think she was renting and, if she did, it would have implications for capital gains tax she'd need to pay when the house sold. It wasn't personal, it was business, but I thought she was being a bit paranoid. I was a friend, and who said I couldn't stay there to help her with Miel and the property? But I wasn't the one negotiating a house sale in France, nor paying taxes according to French law. I was having enough trouble trying to negotiate my own sale in the States.

I'd gone to Apt to do a few errands and ran into Susan. Michael was shopping, so she had time for a cup of coffee at our favorite Aptois café. As we were sipping and chatting, I talked to her about Meg's reluctance to have anyone staying at the house, lest it be construed she was renting. Susan was familiar with the severity of French tax laws and said she wasn't surprised at Meg's hesitancy.

The next afternoon my phone rang. "Jo Anne, it's Susan. How are you?"

"Fine, Susan, it was nice to see you yesterday. I forgot to ask you how Pussycat and Orlando are doing?"

"They're fine, same as always. That's partly why I'm calling. I was telling Michael about the conversation we had yesterday. We wondered if you'd be interested in moving into our apartment when you leave Gary's house. We'd like to take a short trip sometime, and you could have the apartment quid pro quo for a bit of cat- and house-sitting."

I could hardly believe my ears. "Oh, Susan, that would be ideal. You know how much I enjoy the cats, and the apartment is perfect."

"Well, it would work for all of us, and you are welcome to stay on here until you head back to the States at the end of May."

I was thrilled and expressed my gratitude for their generosity, assuring her I would be willing to pay rent for the extended weeks. She insisted they'd be happy to have me there, no remuneration necessary.

176

I hung up the phone and could hardly contain myself. I was relieved and overjoyed! I could look forward to the remainder of my stay in France without worry over venue *or* expense. All because I'd met a friend by chance for a cup of coffee.

March 4, 2014

Anne called yesterday. I'll stay the day and feed the cats, then head back to Gary's in Saignon. Everything has fallen into place for April and May. Melissa is okay to keep Beemer, so I'm good to stay at Michael and Susan's.

I WAS SET FOR THE REMAINDER of my time in France, but I did not have the summer (assuming the condo sale went through) settled, and I didn't know about the following winter or longer, if all went well. I was clinging to my dream of another year in Provence.

Gary had indicated he and Cathy were "going to be using the house differently" in the coming winter. (Which I thought translated into, "Don't plan on coming back, Jo Anne.") Truth be told, it was fun while it lasted, but it had lasted longer than it was fun. I was ready to give up fighting for a parking place, climbing multiple flights of stairs, cleaning an enormous house, worrying about a capricious heating system, and feeling as if my efforts were unappreciated. Why did people like Lizzie and Gary always behave as if they were doing me a favor?

March weather improved, and Meg called saying she'd invited Elizabeth for a short walk, then lunch, and asked me to join them. I thought back to that first winter, 2004, when Lizzie had introduced me to Elizabeth! We hadn't seen a lot of each other in recent years, but I counted her as a friend.

The following day, she and I joined Meg, walked Miel, then helped with yard work. A little later, Meg went to finish lunch while I chatted with Elizabeth as we pulled the overgrowth of weeds along the stone steps leading down to the apartment. Had it really been ten years since we first met? I'd known her longer than I'd known some of my neighbors in Traverse City. We finished the weeding just as Meg called us to have lunch on the terrace. It was a warm day, and I savored the weather, the food, and the warmth of friendships.

March 12, 2014

Sue's emails are increasingly frustrating. I finally called Pete and we had a good talk. The ball is in her court, but she seems to think SHE is in charge and is asking Pete to do all the legal legwork. She hasn't even signed a purchase agreement!!! Pete says (and I concur) her confidence borders on arrogance.

SEVERAL DAYS LATER, Meg called to say Elizabeth was in the hospital in Avignon. She'd had a heart attack and they'd put in a stent. I was shocked! Hadn't we just been weeding the garden together? Meg and I visited the hospital, and seeing her helped me put things in perspective. I renewed my vow to be mindful and healthy and to be where I wanted to be … in France! But I had the summer to go and did not yet know where I'd live once the condo sold. Then I had an idea.

Since I planned to return to France in the fall, why not ask Melissa if she would like a housemate for a few months? We'd been housemates in the past with no overwhelming issues. It would solve my housing conundrum, and it would help Melissa financially. I emailed her my proposal; she thought it was a great plan, and my problem was solved. Once I moved out of the condo, I would move into Melissa's house with her and Beemer. We'd flip-flopped our previous arrangement. I would be a housemate in *her* house.

Pete was doing his best to handle Sue and the condo sale, but he had his own life and business to take care of. One day I phoned Joe and Sally and was telling Joe about the situation.

"Jo Anne," Joe said, "Call Rob and tell him you have a buyer, you have a purchase agreement, and you just need someone to walk the process through to conclusion. He did such a good job selling your place in Glen Arbor. Ask him."

"Do you think he'd do that?" I countered.

"I don't see why not," Joe replied. "Ask him if he'd take three percent to see it through. You've already done all the work. He doesn't have to invest in advertising or showing."

"Brother, you are a genius." I thanked him profusely, and after we chatted for a while, I hung up the phone and sent an email to Rob. I was relieved when Rob sent a reply agreeing to work with Pete and Sue.

41 More Possibilities

WALKING IN APT ONE DAY, I ran into Alexis, a young woman I'd met via Andrew, the owner and chef of the *Petite Cave* restaurant in Saignon. We'd talked on several occasions, and she knew I was on the lookout for affordable year-round housing when I came back to France in the fall. She was well connected with the local population, mentioned a couple of possibilities, and told me she'd follow up and let me know. The next day, Alexis emailed that she had a lead on a house for rent in Buoux.

The tiny village of Buoux was just below the Claparèdes, not far from the Domaine where I'd first stayed and later lived while caring for Lizzie and Andrew's property. The locale had always been a favorite of mine, although the name itself was almost impossible for a speaker of English to pronounce. It came out sounding something like *bwuh-ox.*

The village sat on the edge of a valley, which dipped down to the Aigue Brun River. I remembered relocating stray cats from the Claparèdes to the barn adjacent to a hotel there catering to rock climbers. I thought about the tiny family restaurant that used to be there. I'd always had a special place in my heart for Buoux and the valley. I recalled the feelings of déjà vu I often experienced when I had occasion to go there. Was Buoux calling to me?

A day later, Alexis sent me the owner's phone number, and I made a call. The woman was very French, very friendly, and we arranged for me to visit.

March 27, 2014

I visited the house in Buoux, and I love it! It just feels "right" and "good." I am so excited. Question will be the cost, rent, and utilities, but I think we can work it out. I told the owners I wanted to come back for a second visit, and I'll ask Laurie to go with me.

AS I AWAITED FURTHER DETAILS from the owners of the Buoux house, I could hardly contain my excitement. It felt so right, and I just prayed the cost of the utilities would not be excessive. I wanted it to be the answer to my search.

Life's uncertainties … Stephen's death, Elizabeth's heart attack. I needed to finalize the condo sale and spend another year in Provence.

The packing and leaving process worked on me emotionally. I was mulling the possibility of the little house in Buoux, but wasn't sure I could afford to rent it. I was waiting for the owners to give me an idea of the monthly costs for electricity, phone, TV, internet hookup, taxes, and other fixed expenses. Those costs were charged directly from the providing company to the renter, and the owners were not sure they had records from previous tenants.

April 5, 2014

What a morning!!! I woke to an email from Sue. She has a cash offer on her house and bam!!! She'll buy the condo, but she wants this! She wants that! AND wants possession on June 14th. She's crazy….no grasp of reality.

I WAS GRATEFUL AND RELIEVED Rob had agreed to take over the condo sale and work with Pete. I knew they'd have my interests at heart and was so glad they were on the scene, because I could no longer deal directly with Sue.

As I prepared to leave the Saignon house, I sorted items in kitchen cupboards, cleaned the fireplace, and vacuumed and mopped floors on all four levels. Gary wanted me to check on the house the following week, so at least I didn't have to totally clear out now, and I could get the rest of my things then.

I got a new purchase agreement from Sue's realtor, and the question of possession was problematic. First, she wanted immediate possession, then it was June 14. I was due back in Michigan by May 28, and two weeks would not be enough time for me to recover from jet lag and pack up an entire condo's worth of stuff. The woman was out of touch with reality. I told Rob the date was out of the question. Let him earn his commission by changing it, because I was exhausted.

The following week, Rob emailed saying Sue had an inspection of the condo and was unhappy with the state of the front door and the wood trim around it. She was demanding I have it repaired. The area had been a problem due to a flaw in the builder's design, but I'd had eaves troughs and a drain installed a couple of years earlier, and the issue of water seeping into the trim around the door had been fixed. Yes, if you looked you could see some water stains on the flashing around the door, but they were old, and the problem had been eliminated.

When I'd quoted Sue a price for the condo, it was with the belief that this would be a sale by owner with no realtor commission or other fees involved. As it was, I'd already paid Pete to hold her hand and try to work with her, and when that wasn't sufficient, I'd gotten Rob on board. True, Rob was charging me less than his usual percentage for handling a sale, but it was costing me money, and I had absolutely no intention of spending more to make the sale happen. I had reached my breaking point, and I told Rob to tell Sue I would absolutely not be making any repairs. If she wanted them done, she could jolly well arrange to have them done and pay for them herself.

If my decision was a deal breaker, so be it. I almost wished she'd back out.

April 26, 2014

What a difference a day makes! I'm going to take the house in Buoux!! Laurie went with me, and because she'd overseen the restoration of the property she owned with the Brit couple, she's well versed on restoration. She took photos, examined all of the electric, heating, plumbing, and finish work. The house had originally been a barn attached to the owner's own house, and Laurie says they did a masterful job of renovation. They've used quality materials, and the workmanship was great. A big plus is they are interior decorators, so the finish work with paint, tiles in the kitchen, and bathroom are extremely tasteful and attractive.

I WAS SO EXCITED I could hardly contain myself! At long last, it appeared my dream of spending another year in Provence was becoming a reality … in my own little house. To add to my excitement, I'd managed to work out the timing with the owners. I wouldn't be back until September, and I'd worried they'd want me to sign a lease starting payments immediately. But sometimes they used the little house for overflow of their summer guests and grandchildren, so the timeline was fine with them. With a verbal agreement and handshake, it was done. They even said they'd have handrails put on the stairs leading from the main floor up to the bathroom and bedroom.

The next day, I went to help Meg with yard work and walk Miel. Sadly for Meg, the German couple had backed out of buying the house. After all their demands and contingencies, they suddenly cited a family illness and said they were no longer interested. Meg had wasted more than three months with them and their proposal. She was extremely discouraged and said she couldn't face putting the house back on the market.

I got an email from Sue saying she wanted to buy some of the furniture in the condo, which was good news because I'd have much less to store. I'd learned Traverse City storage units were completely full, a possibility that had not even entered my mind. I'd put my name on the waiting list at a couple of places, since there wasn't much else I could accomplish long-distance, and reasoned that I could take care of it more easily once I was there. At this point in my life, this was my karma: Just when I thought I had smooth sailing, a big wave would wash over the bow.

Sue finally came down off her high horse and signed a purchase agreement allowing me stay in the condo for a month after closing. Of course, she was asking an obscene amount of rent for the month, but I decided to choose my battles, and this wasn't one worth fighting.

On my last day, I said good-bye to Michael and Susan and thanked them profusely for their generosity in providing me a place to stay. I took my car to Meg's, where it would spend the summer. Since a break-in and robbery a few years previously, Meg liked having an extra car around as evidence someone was living there, even though she might be away. She drove me to Avignon, where we hugged and said good-bye at the TGV station.

Au Revoir France, just for now, and onward Jo Anne!

42 Home Sweet Home No More

GRETCHEN PICKED ME UP at Traverse City's Cherry Capital Airport the evening of May 28. She'd moved to her new combination business and studio apartment, so I had the condo to myself.

The closing on the condo sale was set for the very next day. Sue had pushed, and I'd agreed. Rob came to the condo, and together we walked down the street, where we were to meet Sue and her realtor at the title company office. I was in a fog … tired, jet-lagged, and not in the best frame of mind as I anticipated finally meeting the woman who had caused me so much angst.

"Jo Anne! How nice to see you," Sue shrieked, as she jumped up from the chair where she'd been seated and threw her arms around me.

"Yes," I managed to blurt, "nice to meet you at last." I stiffened and hoped my disgust wasn't obvious.

Rob and I took our seats on the other side of a long table facing Sue, her realtor, and the title company officer. Without much ado, the papers were passed around and multiple signatures applied. Less than an hour later, we walked out the door, and I was no longer a homeowner. As Rob and I walked back to the condo, I thanked him for having stepped in, and he assured me he'd be around until I finally moved out at the end of the month. If I needed him, I could call.

I had to pack and get out of the condo. I went around, priced furniture, and made a list. I sold a couple of pieces to Gretchen for her new place, and my neighbor bought the dining-room baker's rack. Sue came by, and I stuck to a very business-like tone of conversation. She agreed to buy a lot of the furniture, which was great. If she detected my cool demeanor, she didn't let on.

A few days after my return, I walked down the street to my chiropractor's office for an adjustment. I'd been going to George for more than ten years and swore by his technique of applied kinesiology as well as his holistic approach to treating the body. As we chatted, I shared with him what I had learned about the lack of storage space in Traverse City.

"Jo Anne," he said. "Don't worry about it. The entire back of this building is a big warehouse, and I'm only using a tiny part of it. My sister had her things stored here before she moved, and you are welcome to the space."

I resisted the urge to jump off the adjustment table and give him a huge hug. Knowing the space was available was such a relief! "George, I can't thank you enough. This is an enormous load off my mind. I'm happy to pay you for the space, just let me know."

"You don't owe me anything," he replied. "Just pay it forward someday." No matter how much I insisted, he insisted more. Not only was he saving me time and worry, he would be saving me a lot of money.

A week after signing the final sale papers, I went out to look at the gardens around the condo, which were a mess. Winter had not been kind to them, and Gretchen hadn't had time for gardening. I wandered out to the condo mailboxes, which were on a main street attached to a wooden platform on a post. I had never had mail delivered there, mostly because I was gone so much, and also because the mailboxes were not locked. The street was a major thoroughfare, and in winter the snowplows were a danger to the mailboxes, as were the fairly sizeable number of homeless people who routinely walked past. I'd opted for the security of a post office box at the local branch. Out of curiosity, I looked into the box assigned to my condo. I was shocked to see a stack of mail. When I pulled it out and looked at it, I saw it was all addressed to Sue. She was already having her mail delivered there! Never mind that she was not entitled to possession until July 1. I was livid. I still lived there, and I was paying a whopping amount of rent for the privilege. She might have owned the place, but I wasn't going to collect her mail.

It was yet more of her arrogant, self-centered attitude. I sent her an email saying she had mail, I would leave it on the back porch for her to collect, and advised her, for reasons of security, that she'd be better served to have a post office box as I had done for years. I told her I would not be collecting any more mail from the box and resisted adding — "So if you want your mail delivered here, you can damned well come and get it yourself!"

Maybe my anger with Sue was a good thing. It kept me from being too nostalgic about saying goodbye to my Woodmere Cottage condo. I'd chosen the lot, watched the house being built, and added my touches during and after construction. I'd shared the process with Rod, and we'd greeted new co-owners as the remaining six houses were finished and sold. The condo had been perfect for summers when I came back from France. From January 10, 2004, to May 29, 2014, I'd called it home sweet home, but … life's choices … it was time to move on.

I'd decided against bringing Beemer to the condo for the month, because cats get upset when you start rearranging furniture, and I knew the condo was going to be a chaotic place until I moved. Melissa wanted to visit relatives for a few days, and I offered to stay at her house with Beemer. Since Melissa had agreed to take me in as a summer housemate after the sale of the condo, this would be a perfect opportunity to get acquainted with her house. On top of that, there'd be no need to find someone to check on Beemer. I finished some packing and went to her house.

Melissa's guest bedroom was pleasant with light-darkening shades and an extremely comfortable bed. I crawled in that night, smiled as I felt Beemer hop up and snuggle at my feet, and wondered how my buddy Sebastian was doing back in France.

As I divested myself of furnishings, some of my more treasured pieces found a new home with Melissa, just as Snowy and Beemer had done. Several original paintings by local artists fit perfectly with Melissa's guest-room theme of the Sleeping Bear Dunes National Lakeshore. I was happy to pass these things on to her and also know, for the next couple of months, that I'd have familiar pieces around me.

I hauled clothes and extra household items to Goodwill and The Father Fred Foundation. I was ashamed to admit I felt reluctant to do my usual donations to Father Fred, because Sue was in charge of the volunteers there! I assumed she was good at what she did, and maybe this was the genesis of her bossy, take-charge way of handling things. I wasn't going to punish the organization because their volunteer director was obnoxious.

June 24, 2014

I dug up some ground cover from my gardens and took them over to Melissa's for her back yard. Got two emails from Sue prodding about when I'll be out of the condo. Pete and Rob advise me to ignore her.

ALL MONTH, I'D BEEN SURROUNDED with boxes and general chaos, but gradually it disappeared, and the last day of the month arrived. The movers came in the morning, and the boxes, along with what few furnishings remained, were now stored in the warehouse behind the chiropractor's office.

Sue had asked for a walk-through of the condo on July first, which Rob assured me was a common request, but not one I was obligated to fulfill. The afternoon of June 30, I took the last of my clothes over to Melissa's but left my iPad and a box of personal items in the kitchen to pick up later in the day. I locked the door and left for Melissa's to have a late lunch with Beemer.

That afternoon, I went back to get my iPad, the box, and for a last-minute check. When I went to unlock the back door, it wouldn't open. I was puzzled, then suddenly realized the deadbolt had been locked. I never locked the deadbolt during the day if I were only going to be gone a short while, and I knew I had not locked it when

I left to go to Melissa's. I suddenly realized the only explanation was that Sue had been there and been inside! Just as I was turning around, she suddenly appeared in the guest parking area of the carports right outside the back porch.

"I'm just leaving the car here," she said. "Someone is picking me up."

I turned and went inside. I was so angry, I was shaking. How dare she! I called Rob and told him what had happened. He was as dumbfounded as I and suggested I send her an email saying we would not be meeting her in the morning for a walk through. I sent the message, carefully refraining from adding any of the number of not nice things I felt like saying. I could have made a legal issue of it had I wanted to, but I was done. I emailed Sue where I would leave the key hidden in the storage shed. Good riddance! If she had any last-minute questions, she was on her own. I locked the door and said goodbye to my Woodmere Cottage. It had been a good home, and I was moving on.

43 The Best-Laid Plans

THE CONDO SALE BEHIND ME, I settled in with Melissa and Beemer. My head and heart were full of conflicting thoughts and emotions. I was elated the condo was sold. I was sad the condo was sold. I was excited about the prospects of at last having my very own place in France. I was apprehensive about having my very own place in France. I loved Northern Michigan in the summer. I hated Northern Michigan in the summer. Well … not exactly hated, but it was not an easy season to be there.

July in Traverse City was chaotic. There was the Fourth of July influx of tourists, with the overlapping annual Cherry Festival events, parades, and carnival rides. Ice-cream-cone-licking tourists sporting flip-flops had a habit of leaving their best manners still packed in the suitcase. They were a disaster behind the wheel of a car, seeming always to be lost, and not bothering to pull over to the side of the road before consulting the map. I decided I'd go out to Joe and Sally's for a couple of days and stay out of the fray. Their peaceful abode in the country outside of Empire would give me a break from the chaos.

On July 3, I went to Munson Medical Center for my annual mammogram. I'd been having mammograms for years, so scheduling one more was no big deal. I read the flyers on the table in the waiting area while the technician took my x-rays back for the doctor to say they were clear enough to study and waved me on. I stepped out onto the parking lot just as the U.S. Navy's Blue Angels, visiting for the National Cherry Festival, went screaming above the hospital and jetting out over Grand Traverse Bay. I turned the car toward Joe and Sally's. Get me out of here!

July 7, 2014

Back in TC after a very nice weekend with Joe and Sally. It's a bit of an odd feeling that I really have no "home," but I'm keeping my eyes on the goal. My own house and my own Year in Provence.

I ENJOYED WORKING IN MELISSA'S GARDENS, and she was appreciative of my efforts. We shared grocery shopping and meal responsibilities, which worked just as well as it had when we were housemates at the condo.

I loved being around Beemer, and the housework and gardens kept me busy, but I kept thinking … not too many more weeks, and I'd be off to France and my little house in Buoux. I already had plans of how I would plant flowers on the spacious patio overlooking the valley and where I'd put my desk and computer for writing. I fantasized enjoying a glass of wine on the terrace. I could just feel Buoux calling me.

The following week, I got a call saying I needed to have a follow-up mammogram. This time the doctor wanted me to go to the Copper Ridge Breast Center, just west of town, and had me scheduled for a re-take on July 18. I had it done and went on my way. I put that behind me and kept thinking about the Buoux house, visualizing how I was going to make my nest.

My enthusiasm diminished when I got a call from the breast center saying I needed to come back, this time for a needle biopsy. They had found something in my left breast. I was more annoyed than worried, but the biopsy wasn't scheduled until the end of the month, so there didn't appear to be any urgency.

WHEN THE TWO OF US had gone for my second visit to the house in Buoux, Laurie had taken photos, and I kept dragging them out. I dreamed of making meals in the tiny but beautifully appointed kitchen, with its classy white-and-blue-tiled countertops, and then sitting with my morning coffee on the large terrace gazing over the lavender fields in the valley below. It was a daily daydream.

July 26, 2014

Woke with a painful stiff neck. I called George, and he's going to fit me in. I just want to be healthy and done with all these medical issues. Got an email from the owners of the Buoux house. We're set to meet September 5th.

MY LIVING ARRANGEMENT with Melissa meant I was able to be with Beemer. He was getting to be an old man for sure, but he was playful and eating well. It was time for his annual checkup. My vet, Dr. Everett, had retired the year before, but he'd brought in a very nice female veterinarian.

The new vet gave Beemer a good exam and was astounded at his overall health as well as the excellent results of his kidney function and other tests. But he was aging, and we talked about what it was going to mean someday down the road.

Thursday, August 31, I went to the breast center for the needle biopsy. I'd need to come back the following Tuesday for the results of the biopsy. I left the center and headed to Joe and Sally's for a weekend of fresh country air and family time.

Joe and Sally had put their house on the market just a few months earlier. They'd enjoyed their time in The Villages in Florida and were looking toward retirement. They were more than ready to be done with ice, snow, and sleet-slicked roads between their house in Empire and schools in Traverse City. A possible sale of their house didn't affect me directly, but it was one more element of change in the offing.

On Tuesday, August 5, my appointment at Copper Ridge was at 2:30 p.m. I was feeling great and eager to get on with things. One month to go, and I'd be in France! A nurse took me into a small consultation room and seated me at a round table. There were stacks of flyers and folders on the table, a computer, printer, and phones on a desk. The door opened, and a very friendly female doctor came in with a folder under her arm. She introduced herself, shook my hand, took a seat laying the folder on the table and said, "Well, it's cancer."

I'm not sure what I said, if anything, in response. I suppose she'd learned there was no gentle way to give someone bad news. She proceeded to explain it wasn't a large tumor, just one centimeter, the size of a pea, but it needed to come out. (No argument from me on that score.) After a few perfunctory remarks, she exited the room, leaving me in the hands of a very kind and compassionate nurse.

I spent the better part of an hour with the nurse, who made an appointment for me to see a surgeon. She proceeded to wade through papers, folders, flyers, and all manner of explanations about breast cancer, what the various treatments could be after surgery including information about cancer support groups, wigs for che-motherapy-induced balding heads, and statistics on survival rates. I couldn't help but think this must be a pro-forma spiel … she already had me lined up for support groups and a wig! What about just taking it out and being merrily on my way? I was polite, not pleased. She was, after all, just doing her job. I tucked the papers under my arm and left.

Once in the car, I called Joe and Sally with the news. They were as astounded as I, but reassured me they'd do whatever I needed. Suddenly, I was really happy to be in Michigan—close to my family.

On Friday, I went to Joe and Sally's and planned to stay with them until Tuesday, when Joe would go with me to meet the surgeon. I appreciated their support and was glad to be in the country, away from the Traverse City's busy-ness.

The surgeon proved to be a perfectly charming young woman (and I do mean YOUNG), and I liked her a lot. Even Joe, with his general dislike and distrust of doctors, felt comfortable with her. She went over everything in detail and said she'd see us at the hospital the following week.

I sent Meg an email, told her about the cancer, and asked her to keep it under her hat; but I should have known the ex-pat Luberon drums would beat out the message. I got an email from Gary, saying he knew I'd wanted to keep things quiet but …. In a sense I appreciated the caring.

On the nineteenth, Joe took me to Munson Medical Center, where I was checked in, assigned a bed, and Joe kept close by in a family waiting area. I could not have been more pleased with the way the nurses and technicians treated me, and him. Under odious circumstances, I was made comfortable physically and emotionally. Nurses wheeled my gurney to a pre-op arena, where nice people gave me warm blankets, asking me repeatedly if I was okay.

The next thing I recalled was a blur of masked faces leaning over me and waking to realize one of them was my surgeon, who didn't look much like she did in the office, now garbed in surgical scrubs, wearing a cap, with a mask hanging down from her chin. I do remember her telling me everything went well. Gradually, I regained most of my senses, and there was Joe at my bedside. My brother had never looked so good! In the afternoon, I was wheeled out to the car, and Joe took me home with him.

August 24, 2014

What a week (almost) it's been!! But I got the call late Friday that the cancer is gone! I've been on a roller coaster since the surgery, but now I'm on to Plan B, which means staying in Michigan until October.

A WEEK AFTER THE SURGERY, Joe and I went to see the surgeon. She told us the surgery had taken longer than expected because after removing the tumor and sending it to the lab, she had not been happy with the way the surrounding tissue looked, and she went back in to take out more. She assured us the margins around the tumor were completely clear as were the lymph glands.

In the true allopathic style of modern medicine, I was scheduled for follow up with radiologists and oncologists. They were not rec-ommending chemotherapy, but they were suggesting possible radia-tion, and, since my tumor had been estrogen positive, a medication to prevent my body from producing estrogen. To their credit, they were all keenly aware I was having to delay my return to France and were seeking ways for me to get any treatment I might opt to undergo as expeditiously as possible.

I met with the oncologist and with the radiologist. Ultimately, I decided against the radiology, and they really didn't insist. I agreed to get the prescription filled for the estrogen-inhibiting drug but did not begin taking it. I consulted my acupuncturist, who had done internships at the Mayo Clinic and who was an expert in Chinese medicine, and talked with George, my chiropractor, who did some muscle testing with the drug. We blind tested it among a number of other supplements and medications, and my body repeatedly indi-cated it did NOT like the drug.

I could not have had a more supportive group of friends. In France, Anne, Susan, and another ex-pat, Amanda, were breast cancer survi-vors. I had to admit to being surprised at Anne's information. I had known about Sue's and Amanda's experience, but not Anne's.

It was helpful to me to hear from Amanda saying she had tried the estrogen-inhibiting drug and had experienced horrific side effects. Those possible side effects had been described to me and, along with George's muscle testing, were what ultimately led me to decide against the drug. My rationale was this: My surgeon said the tumor had been completely removed. The margins around the area were clear. The lymphs were clear. I did not have cancer. Why would I want to behave as if I DID and take radiation? Or behave as if I feared a possible recurrence and take drugs? I did neither.

I'd emailed the owners of the house in Buoux to say I would not be back in France until October and was unsure if I would be able to follow up on the rental of the house. They assured me they were in no hurry to rent, and we agreed to stay in touch once I got back to France. Meg, in her customary compassionate and helpful manner, offered to have me come and rent her apartment. After weeks and weeks of upheaval, I finally saw a proverbial light at the end of that legendary long and dark tunnel, but not before I had my moments when I wanted to have an all-out temper tantrum.

Inside I was furious. How dare the Universe mess with my plans … just when I was, at long last, about to realize my dream of having my very own place in Provence? All mine, and in a location that had always been so special. I had been set to move to Buoux, to sit on the terrace, to gaze over the valley covered with fields of lavender. I was beyond disappointed and more than just a little pissed off!

It was September. When I should have been winging my way to France, I was struggling to heal from surgery and regain my emotional equilibrium.

I tried to rest and heal, but my body had not responded well to the anesthetic, and I fought vertigo and fatigue. I exercised, got acupuncture treatments, and rested, but it wasn't easy. Melissa had plans to go on a three-week trip to Australia to visit a friend with a stop on the way to see relatives in California. I would take care of Beemer and have three weeks in the house on my own, which would be good for healing my body, mind, and spirit.

44 Losing A Friend

September 14, 2014

I got an email from Melissa that she arrived safely in California. She'll be there until Monday, when she leaves for Australia. Didn't sleep too well last night because Beemer was restless.

THE MORNING OF SEPTEMBER 19, I woke with a feeling something wasn't right. Beemer always slept on my bed (or on Melissa's when she was there.) That morning he wasn't there, nor did he come running when I got up and went to the bathroom, so I grabbed my bathrobe and started looking. I found him in the living room hunched up behind a chair and in obvious distress.

I watched as he wandered around, straining as if to have a bowel movement, but nothing was happening. Then, suddenly, he began to vomit, and as he did he had a bout of diarrhea. It was barely eight o'clock, but I knew the vet's office would be open, and I called. The technician said to bring Beemer in at ten o'clock.

I spent the next hour trying to keep Beemer comfortable and clean. He'd completely lost control of his bowels and was vomiting periodically. Finally, at nine thirty, I put him into his carrier and then in the car. I wasn't going to call the vet's office; I was just going to go. Surely, when they saw how sick he was, they'd see him immediately.

Once we arrived, I didn't have long to wait. We were ushered into an examining room, and one of the vet assistants came in. I explained to her what was going on, and she proceeded to examine him. When she tried to insert a thermometer, she turned to me and said, "He's completely constipated. He's blocked. We'll probably have to give him an enema, but I'll wait for the doctor."

The same pleasant female vet we'd seen in August came into the room. "What's going on?" she queried. I explained how I'd found him when I got up, and how ill he was. I also mentioned the technician's diagnosis of constipation. She took Beemer into her hands, and gently began examining his stomach and sides. After a few minutes, she stopped and looked up at me. "He's not constipated, Jo Anne, he has a large mass in his stomach. It's completely blocking his intestines and organs, and that's why he's struggling to move his bowels and it's causing the vomiting. I suppose … (and she hesitated) I could try surgery." I just looked at her. "We talked about this when I was here last month," I said. "No surgery." I didn't need to say more. "Wait here," she said, "I'll be back in a few minutes."

I just sat there. Part of me knew this was inevitable, yet I was stunned.

When she came back into the room carrying Beemer, she'd inserted an injection line into his leg. "I've given him a sedative, he's relaxed and almost asleep." Indeed, he was limp and breathing calmly. She handed him to me. "You hold him. I'm going to give him the injection. He may wince, but it is just the body's reaction, he's not feeling anything." And so I held him as we watched. After a few minutes, she put the stethoscope to his body, listened, and nodded.

"Do you want to have him cremated?" I nodded yes. I handed his lifeless body back to her. "Just go on home, there's no need to stop at the desk. We'll be in touch."

I picked up the empty carrier and walked out of the office into the September sunlight.

September 20, 2014

…. A storm in the wee hours. Lots of rain. I'm feeling so sad over losing Beemer but relieved he didn't suffer. I connected with Melissa on Face-

Time last night and shared the news. She was shocked and sad. I put all the cat things in the car and will take them to the Humane Society.

THE FOLLOWING WEEK, I struggled. I was bereft at losing Beemer. The days grew more autumnal … my most un-favorite time of year. Colder nights, shorter days, and I grew shorter and shorter on patience. Condo sale, cancer surgery, Beemer gone … I wanted to put all of this behind me … I wanted to be in France! Why had the Universe conspired to shatter my plans? To hand me cancer and to rip away my dear pet? I fought off depression and spent a lot of time in tears.

On the second of October, I had a final meeting with the surgeon. I explained my decision not to take the estrogen-inhibiting medication, and she didn't argue with me. After examining the incision, she said it was healing nicely. I thanked her profusely for her expertise and caring. "And please don't take it personally," I said, as I exited the examining room, "but I hope I won't be seeing you again."

She smiled and waved her hand.

MELISSA RETURNED FROM HER TRIP to Australia. The vet's office called, and I went to pick up Beemer's cremains, in the sweet paw-printed container with accompanying papers of poems and cards, which I shared with Melissa. Neither of us had the heart to do anything with the ashes at the time, so she placed them in a safe corner of a cabinet.

45 Back to the Familiar

WITH THE ALL CLEAR FROM THE SURGEON, I called the airlines to reschedule my flight. I had to pay a hefty change fee, but wonder of wonders, when I explained the reason for my delayed departure, the agent waived the additional penalty fee with no documentation required.

With the airline ticket purchased, I felt a sense of relief … at last a departure date. Clearly my life was never going to be without challenges, but my energy was returning, as was my positive outlook.

The owners of the property in Buoux had sent a message saying they were not in a hurry to rent the little house, meaning I could hold on to the option of moving there the following spring. This would give me time to be based at Meg's yet spend a December to February at Paul and Anne's house while they went to England and South Africa. Maybe by spring, I'd regain my equilibrium and be ready for more independence. My own nest in Buoux went on the back burner. I did my best to make the most of reality.

During the week, I mailed boxes to France, visited Joe and Sally for a couple of days to say goodbye, and then, on October 28, said *au revoir* to Melissa and Michigan.

November 2, 2014 At Meg's

A long trip but so happy to be here. Laurie picked me up at the TGV and Meg had supper for us. It feels so good to be back in this familiar apartment. Meg has ordered firewood, and the chimney sweep is coming.

JOE AND SALLY HAD THEIR HOUSE on the market, and just before I left Michigan, they told me they thought they had a buyer. I got periodic messages from them, and it looked as if their buyer was going to be Sue, reincarnated. I could commiserate but hoped the outcome would be in their favor.

Life took on a familiar rhythm. Meg and I walked Miel around the vineyard and the lavender fields on the Claparèdes. I mapped out plans with Paul and Anne for my winter house- and cat-sitting.

In mid-November, they stopped by to discuss Sebastian's health. Dear Sebby's ears and nose were covered with large sores and scabs. We knew they were cancerous, but they'd decided against any surgeries and the treatment was to keep them clean and clear of infection. In anticipation of their extended time away during the upcoming months, they wanted to ensure I was comfortable handling Sebby's treatment and, should it become necessary, would take him for euthanasia. I promised them I was up for the task, whatever it might turn out to be, while secretly hoping not to have a repeat of losing Beemer.

Meg asked me what I wanted to do for my birthday and offered to fix lunch. I really did not want to focus on turning seventy-eight years old. *Old.* That's how it sounded to me. But I didn't feel old, and wasn't I the one always saying, "It's just a number?"

I suggested we keep it simple, so we invited Laurie and Elizabeth to join us for lunch, and at my request, Meg fixed another one of my favorite dishes, *lapin à la moutarde.* I remember eating rabbit as a little girl, after my dad had gone hunting with my Uncle Al. Americans weren't big on rabbit, but it was fairly common in France. I remember Meg telling me if she had a picky American eater or two among a group she'd invited for a meal, she'd pass rabbit off as Provençal chicken. In truth, you could hardly tell the difference. I felt happy, warm, and content sharing my special day with good food and close friends ... in France. There'd been big celebrations for my seventieth and seventy-fifth, and smaller ones with simple fare at the Claparèdes, and fettuccini alfredo with Stephen. Gosh, what a history of birthdays in France!

That evening, I sat quietly pondering. This had not been the best of years for me. I reminded myself that it's always better to look ahead, not back. I was more than ready for a new year.

46 Shifting Emotions

I WAS ALWAYS EAGER to welcome in a new year. This year more than ever. I'd really struggled to regain my emotional equilibrium after the events of 2014. I felt as if it had been a year of loss … of major change. I no longer owned a house. I'd made it through a bout of breast cancer, but it had left me feeling vulnerable. I was so accustomed to being in perfect health. The doctors always told me I was in extraordinarily good health, sometimes adding, "For your age." Why did they need to keep reminding me of my age? I'd be damned if I was going to succumb to the generally accepted state of being "old." I had things I wanted to do and experiences yet to be enjoyed.

As if the health issues weren't enough, there was the loss of Beemer. Joe and Sally were leaving Michigan. Some days I felt as if my world had tipped on its axis. All that said, I remained the eternal optimist. I had a good friend years ago who always reminded me, "All things work together for good." Right.

New Year's Day, 2015

A new year! Turn the page! I walked with Meg and Miel yesterday, then spent the rest of the day cleaning the apartment. Meg brought Miel down in the evening so she could go to a New Year's Eve party. I had a quiet evening with Miel and took her upstairs when I headed to bed around 10:30 p.m.

I WAS HAPPY TO BE IN FRANCE but began sensing a shift in my attitude and reactions. It had been a tough summer for me, and my level of tolerance and acceptance of even seemingly small inconveniences was not as high or as strong as it used to be. Was the honeymoon over? What I once considered quaint and unique began to be bothersome … excess calcium in the water, hanging laundry outside to dry, and erratic internet service began to annoy me. Then I'd gazed at the view over the vineyard and feel more content.

January 13, 2015

Back in Roussillon. Sebby's ear is bad again. The vet gave Paul and Anne tranquilizers so if the worst happens and I have to take him to the vet, he'll be sleeping. I pray I won't have to do that.

Paul and Anne left for South Africa, and I resumed my life with the cats. I loved the sunny terrace off the kitchen and, even in January, I could sit out there, read, and look south over the valley to the village of Lacoste. At sunset, as the skies darkened, I could see the lights of the Chateau of the Marquis de Sade twinkling in the distance. This is it! I reminded myself. This sense of history, of permanence and … the amazing beauty of the hills.

January 26, 2015

Got an email yesterday from Anne. They're leaving South Africa and on to London. Really worried about Sebby's nose, yesterday it seemed to bother him a lot.

WHEN WE EXCHANGED EMAILS, I didn't say anything to Paul and Anne about Sebby's nose and ears. I wanted them to enjoy their vacation, and it served no purpose to mention the cat. I hoped

I wasn't ignoring the seriousness of his wounds, but he honestly did not seem to be in pain, was eating well, and behaving normally. Periodically, he would sneeze a lot, and I surmised the growths might be increasing inside his nose, where I could not see them, but then he'd stop, and I'd relax.

February fourth, we had a horrific snowstorm, which broke long-standing records for snowfall in the Luberon. The house was located at the bottom of an extremely steep, paved drive, and there was no way I could get my car out. I had provisions, firewood, and cat food. I didn't need to go anywhere.

I listened to the appalling weather reports, smiling as I remembered those years when I first began coming to the Luberon and would smugly tell people, "Oh, it may snow once or twice, just a little, but it melts in a few hours." This was going to be about the third time in the past eleven or so years I could be called a liar! We had over a foot of heavy, wet snow. Then the temperatures dropped and effectively froze it in place for the remainder of the week.

February 10, 2015

Sebby is doing better. I really worked on cleaning the scabby part on his ear. Ellie brought in a rat/mouse/vol this morning. Yuk! Emails from Anne … they are settled in their London apartment.

DURING THE SECOND WEEK OF FEBRUARY, there were patches of snow on the ground, but the forecast was for rain, which I hoped would wash away the last of the white stuff. Sebby's ear looked better. Maybe it was Sebby's condition and the unusual weather, but I wasn't as relaxed as past times when I'd stayed there.

A couple of days later, the electric company, EDF, sent a notice they'd be shutting off the electricity for a day. It went off at 8:15 a.m. and did not come back on by late afternoon as scheduled. I finally made a phone call and was told the electricity was, indeed, back on, and I should go out to the main box on the road to see if there was a problem there. They said it was obviously my problem, not theirs.

I had no idea what to look for since, in the eight years I'd stayed there, I'd never had any need to go to the box outside. I finally called the nice French man who lived up the lane and who had helped me in the past with the pool. "No, Jo Anne," he assured me, "The electricity is still out." I thanked him and, somewhat reassured, I waited. Sure enough, about an hour later it came on.

Talk about frustrated! Why in the hell would the EDF representative give me erroneous information? It was the government electrical company, for God's sake. It was *Électricité De France!* Didn't they know what was going on? This was the company whose bill was proof you lived in your house … evidence of your very existence, and they didn't know when the electricity was back on?

A few days later, the landline phone and internet went out. When I called the phone company on my mobile phone, I was told our service had been disconnected *"par erreur."* I was incredulous. How do you disconnect someone's service by mistake! I called Meg on my mobile phone and asked her to send Paul and Anne an email.

From London, Anne called the phone company and learned the information I'd received was completely wrong. There'd been a major line disruption in the entire area. The phone and internet finally came back on around 3 p.m.

The next day, Sebby lost another big scabby part of his ear and it bled. I finally got it stopped and bathed it in Betadine. I tried hard to find the lessons in all of this, but I was increasingly frustrated. Snowstorms, electrical outages, a sick cat, internet, and phone out … but I was in France, right?

Be careful what you ask for.

March 7, 2015 Back in Saignon

Paul and Anne returned yesterday afternoon. We had a nice visit. I've turned Sebby over to them. Meg had me up for cottage pie supper when I got back, and we had a good conversation about housing. Now to settle in and feel more permanent. Onward!

A FEW DAYS AFTER THEIR RETURN, I got an email from Anne saying Sebby's condition had worsened to the point where they'd felt he was suffering. My suspicions about the growths in his nose had been confirmed, as he was having trouble breathing and was sneezing constantly. A couple of days later, Paul emailed that they had taken Sebby in and had him euthanized. They'd arranged with the vet to take him on a Sunday morning when there would be no one (other than emergencies) in the clinic and had also given him the tranquilizers.

I was overwhelmed with sadness, but I knew it was for the best. It was doubly hard for me, since I'd just spent such an extended amount of time with him. But over the next week, as we talked and I looked at photos of the cats, I could see how he had deteriorated.

It took many days for me to stop having periodic spells of crying, but as the weather improved, I concentrated on the fact that I was in France for the duration! At last!

47 Back and Forth

SPRING ARRIVED, and I had no house- or pet-sitting obligations other than off and on with Miel, which didn't require moving anywhere. I was *chez moi* … at home.

Joe and Sally emailed they had finalized the sale of their house and filed their retirement papers at the end of the first semester of the school year. They would be moving to The Villages in May.

Finally, there were no loose ends dangling. I was using Melissa's address in Traverse City as my permanent address, giving me a base in the States. I was finally going to enjoy another spring and summer in the Luberon. I looked forward to the scent of lavender in bloom and the sight of fields of sunflowers lifting their faces to the heavens. And, on a more mundane level, there were crunchy baguettes, melt-in-your-mouth croissants, and really good, inexpensive wine!

I was happy as I contemplated my extended time in France, but I didn't feel as overwhelmingly ecstatic as I had thought I would. For a long time, you think you want something; you dream about it, you work hard to make it happen, and when it becomes reality … it just doesn't live up to your vision. I'd always enjoyed my life in France, and I was baffled. When had it become almost "ho-hum?" Where was the thrill? The excitement?

My Luberon routine was familiar: went to Megaform, went to market, shopped, helped Meg in the yard, walked Miel around the

vineyard. I'd been walking Miel around that vineyard since 2004 … eleven years!

I don't know exactly when I started mentally looking around, the way you do when you have a feeling something's lacking, but aren't quite sure what. Was my old nemesis, Restless, creeping up on me? I felt a little like the old Peggy Lee song, "Is That All There Is?"

I churned around with my emotions for a while and decided I'd make a trip to the States before full-on summer arrived in my adopted country. I could take care of medical appointments in Traverse City and then head south to Florida to visit Joe and Sally in their new place.

I'd so anticipated another summer in Provence … lavender, bees, honey, sunflowers, cicadas, heat, and tourists. Tourists! The thought made me realize I needed to go to Traverse City before the town was overrun with them. I emailed Melissa, who said she'd be happy to have me for a visit in June. I planned to get my annual medical checkups and inspect my possessions stored with George. After a week in Traverse City, I'd go to Florida to see Joe, Sally, Will, and … The Villages.

June 1, 2015

I'm at Melissa's in Traverse City! Yesterday's travel was long. Delays in Chicago but finally got here at 10 p.m.

I SPENT A BUSY BUT PLEASANT couple of weeks in Traverse City. We enjoyed cooking together and sharing meals on the terrace. I made the rounds of doctors with good results (fewer comments on my age), shopped, and visited friends. I also took another major step toward freeing myself from stateside obligations by selling my car. Melissa's neighbor needed a different car and wanted to buy hers, so it worked perfectly for her to buy mine. One less tie.

I wrapped up my Michigan stay, said good-bye to Melissa, and left for the flight to Florida.

The following weeks, I enjoyed family time and explored an entirely different lifestyle in The Villages. It was a planned community full of golf courses and tons of activities and clubs designed for energetic senior citizens.

I left for France with my heart full from quality time with Joe and Sally and my head full of possibilities for what might well become my future home base ... some day ... after France. For now, I wanted to bask in the scent of lavender and *ma vie en France.*

June 26, 2015 Meg's apartment

It is going to be HOT! What a great visit I had with Joe and Sally. Meg met my train in Avignon. We had supper on her terrace. Yesterday, the farmer woke me at 7 a.m. spraying in the vineyard below. Meg and I took Miel walking in the lavender fields above Saignon, and Meg took photos of me, knee deep in lavender! Then we went for coffee at Christine's in the village. It feels great!

I WAS REALLY HAPPY ... walking Miel in the vineyard, wading in fields of lavender, sipping kir with Meg, and enjoying morning coffee on my terrace above the vineyard. Each morning, I opened the shutters and gazed at the hills in the distance, now a patchwork of green vineyards and purple lavender fields. I thought back to that first summer, in 2004, when I hadn't had time to savor coffee, kir, or the view. I'd survived, and it was the first chapter in the story of my eleven-year ping-pong existence between Northern Michigan and Southern France.

The following week, I enjoyed a couple of days with the cats in Roussillon. Both Frankie and Ellie hung out in the shade near the house, but I missed Sebby. I'd often turn, expecting to see him sitting near his favorite pot of flowers and tears would fill my eyes.

July temperatures intensified. There's no such thing as central air conditioning in rural France. Electricity is too, too expensive. I purchased a couple of oscillating fans to keep the air in my apartment moving.

I went for coffee at Christine's and markets in nearby villages. This is what I'd been yearning to do, but something was lacking.

As summer intensified, I felt unsettled … and yes, restless. Joe and Sally emailed about their new domicile and what they were doing to get it settled. I thought back to last June's visit and began to think about seeing them. I decided to make another trip back to the States in November, directly to Florida. It would be great to be there for Thanksgiving and my birthday. No more faux Thanksgiving holidays in France; I craved the real thing.

Even with my familiar activities, there were times when I felt I did not fit in. No matter how much I pondered it, I could not put my finger on what had changed. My feelings bothered me, because I was doing exactly what I'd hoped and planned to do, and I had many months ahead of me to enjoy *ma vie en France*.

I shook off the uncomfortable feelings, and went ahead with plans to visit Joe and Sally in November. It felt good to anticipate the trip, after which I'd be heading to Roussillon for extended time with my feline buddies. In the meantime, I did my best to enjoy the autumn weather as I watched the grape harvest, *le vendange*, in the vineyard below the house.

48 Horror

MEG WAS GOING TO TAKE ME to the TGV in Avignon the morning of November 14, 2015, for my trip up to Paris and flights to the States. That morning, I got up and turned on the radio to the news of the terrorist attack and massacre at the Bataclan nightclub in Paris. I was stunned, horrified, dismayed, and incredulous as reality hit me. What an abominable event! During times of war, you heard a casualty count. This wasn't war. This was Paris and these were not soldiers, these were innocent civilians out for a night on the town. I felt sick to my stomach.

I quickly processed the implications for my travel and knew there would be no way I could leave that day. The entire city was in turmoil, and even though the airport was outside of Paris, I knew the security on trains and in the airport itself would be intense, and there would be chaos.

Security and chaos aside, I felt sufficiently unsettled not to want to go anywhere. My adopted country, a country I had grown to know and love, had been attacked. I was heartbroken along with all of France and mourners around the world.

I called the airlines and was easily able to delay my departure by two days with the same itinerary and no penalties. The sixteenth, Meg took me to the TGV in Avignon, and on the seventeenth, I boarded my flight to Orlando.

November 19, 2015 The Villages, Florida

On the screened-in porch of my Villages rental house. Joe and Sally met me at Lake Sumter Landing and took me to the office, where I met the realtor who brought us here. It's a fantastic house, beautifully furnished. Maggie arrives this afternoon for three days. Ongoing news about the Paris terrorist attack. I'm heartsick.

MY LONG-TIME FRIEND, Maggie, lived south of Orlando and planned to come spend a few days with me in The Villages Lifestyle Preview house. Maggie had been with me in France on several occasions dating back to those original artists trips in 2002 and 2003, and she'd visited me the fall of 2006, when I'd stayed in Tim and Mary's house. Not only would I have family time, I'd reconnect with a long-time Stateside friend.

The next two weeks were a whirlwind of feelings, activities, and new experiences. There was much news of the Paris attacks, and just hearing the reports was unsettling. I'd developed such a love for and affinity to France, it was hard not to feel sadness and grief every time I thought about my adopted country. I did my best to put the tragic events aside and focus on my time visiting The Villages.

Joe saw to it that I was comfortable driving into the town center with the golf cart, the major mode of transportation in and around The Villages. It seemed odd not to go everywhere in a car, but hey, I thought, why not?

Maggie arrived, and our time together was superb. Maggie was short with a head of cropped, snow-white hair. At eighty-three years old, she'd survived breast and colon cancer, the loss of her long-time male partner a couple of years earlier, and had not slowed down. We shared not only history, but also a similar positive outlook on life. She was a joy to be with!

As we watched the news, she and I talked about how different it was living in the States than in Europe. Sure, we'd had our 9/11 attack, but somehow feeling comfortable wasn't as easy in France.

Being with Maggie, I realized there's nothing like a connection where you have personal history. As much as I was enjoying my year in Provence, there was something about the familiarity of long-time friends and life in the States that felt good.

The following week, I stayed with Joe and Sally. We shopped, went sightseeing, and relaxed. Thanksgiving Day, Sally set a lovely table with her china and crystal. A sweet potato pie followed Joe's superb stuffed turkey and trimmings (including the green bean mushroom soup casserole, of course!). Four days later, we celebrated my birthday by driving to one of the country clubs known for its buffet breakfast. We had our made-to-order omelet and tasty sweet rolls while sitting on an outside terrace, sipping coffee, and watching the golfers. I loved it!

I enjoyed quality family time with a more in-depth look at The Villages Lifestyle, and it was definitely "a lifestyle." Joe had told me it was impossible to explain, and he was right. It was like stepping into a different world. What impressed me most was the atmosphere of happiness and friendliness. Oh, I was sure there were disadvantages and negatives to be found. Nowhere on earth is the perfect place. Hadn't I come to that realization about life in France?

As I contemplated this lifestyle, I became conscious of the fact that I'd adapted to a way of life in France that differed drastically from the States, and for a time it had been thoroughly enjoyable. I also realized I'd become impatient with the inconveniences. Silly things like curbside pickup of your trash in the States sure beat the French system of hauling stinking trash bags in your car to the closest dumpster. Here there was a garbage disposal, a clothes dryer, reliable TV, and dependable internet! Stores were open seven days a week, and in some cases twenty-four hours a day.

Was I a spoiled American? I didn't think so. Trash, TV, internet, clothes dryers, and convenient shopping were superficialities; my growing discontent with France went deeper. It was hard for me to admit that it was anything but idyllic, yet I couldn't say exactly why I felt a growing discontent. Restless?

I'd assimilated into the customs, culture, and patterns of French life, but did I want to live with them for the rest of my days? It had been twelve years since my first stay in the Luberon. Yes, that part of France had become a part of me, but I wasn't feeling the same sense of excitement and anticipation that I'd felt in the past. Times change, and so do people. Had I?

On the first of December, I said a reluctant good-bye to Joe, Sally, and Will, boarded the shuttle bus to the Orlando airport and, after an overnight there, made my journey back to France.

49 Uncertainty

December 4, 2015

Back in Saignon! It's good to be back in France, but not sure how much longer this will go on. Meg picked me up in Avignon; I unpacked, then went and joined her for supper.

I HAD FOUR DAYS TO RE-GROUP, fight with jet lag, and then went to Roussillon for my pre-Christmas cat care of Ellie and Frankie. I was amazed at how quickly I slid back into *ma vie en France*.

I adjusted, but I wasn't particularly happy. For one thing, the weather turned un-Provençal gray and wet. Secondly, I'd never really enjoyed the Christmas holiday away from my family, and having just spent time with Joe and Sally only amplified the void.

The rain and damp kept Ellie and Frankie inside more than normal. Ellie was particularly needy and often joined me on the sofa in the evening to have her belly rubbed and head scratched. I loved her, but I missed Sebby.

December 14, 2015

Another gray and cloudy morning. Went back to my apartment yesterday. Meg was at her Book Club Christmas Lunch so fed Miel.

I GOT MESSAGES FROM JOE AND SALLY saying long-time friends from Michigan came to visit, and another Michigan couple had rented a house in The Villages for two months. Joe was sounding happier and more settled, which I thought had a lot to do with having contact with old friends. I could relate.

My mind began working on a plan to get back to The Villages. What if I bought a place there and, when I wanted to come spend time in France, rented it out? I emailed Pete, who continued to oversee my finances after the condo sale fiasco with Sue, and ran it by him. He'd give it some thought when the holidays were over and get back to me.

Meg resumed hosting her pre-Christmas party after the year's hiatus following Stephen's death. I left the cats and went to Saignon in the afternoon. I helped her get organized, and as guests arrived, I lit candles and put out food. I chatted with a few folks, hung around long enough to be sociable, and scooted back to my feline buddies and cozy fire.

Later that week, I got an email from Anne. She filled me in on their estimated arrival on the twenty-second, and invited me to come for New Year's Eve. She and Paul had invited Michael and Susan and a woman who owned the house just up the road. It would be a small dinner party with close friends, and she said I could plan to stay overnight in the guest room. I accepted cheerfully. This was more like my idea of welcoming in the New Year!

On the twenty-second, I said *au revoir* to Ellie and Frankie and went to my apartment. I put a few Christmas decorations around the mantle, and the room looked appropriately festive. Meg had bought two lobster tails and suggested she and I have Christmas Eve supper. I'd offered to bring champagne and appetizer. We had both been invited to Christmas Day lunch with Laurie, her two housemates, and a couple of their houseguests. I'd agreed to attend, thinking it would be a small group with some different faces.

Christmas Eve day dawned sunny, and we walked Miel around the vineyard. I'd gone to Apt the day before and splurged on some *foie gras* for us to have as an appetizer before the lobster, and had a bottle of champagne chilling in the fridge. I sent emails to Joe and

Sally wishing them a Merry Christmas. I was relaxing that afternoon when my phone rang, and the caller ID said, "Meg."

"Hi Meg, what's up?"

"I'm sick," came the answer. At first, I thought she was joking. She was fine that morning.

"Why? What's wrong?" I finally managed to ask.

"I don't know, but about a half hour ago I started to have chills and I've had a bout of diarrhea." Her tone wasn't a joking one.

"Oh, Meg, I'm so sorry. What can I do?" I asked.

"Really nothing," she said. "I'll be okay, but I don't think I'm up to foie gras and lobster."

"I understand," I replied. "I'm here; just let me know if you need anything, even if it's the middle of the night. Okay?" I hung up and looked around the room. I was disappointed but there wasn't much to do about it. I decided to light the fire and settle down for the evening. I had food on hand, but I was concerned about Meg, and glad to be close by just in case.

December 26, 2015

Covered sky, warm. Made it through Christmas Day. I walked Miel for Meg but she decided she felt well enough to go to lunch with Laurie's group. It was a nice meal, but we didn't linger. Really feeling closure coming on here … time to move on.

WITH THE POSSIBILITY of less time in France, I needed to get rid of excess, and began to cull through my accumulated belongings. I thought longingly of the sweet little house in Buoux, but that opportunity was gone. I'd given up any idea of renting a house or apartment in France for a long term. Maybe I'd resume my old pattern of a few months here and the rest in the States?

Christmas behind me, I looked forward to New Year's Eve at Paul and Anne's. But mostly, I was looking forward to a really NEW Year.

50 Winding Down

I SPENT THE FIRST WEEK OF 2016 shaking off the holiday ho-ho-ho. I stashed the Christmas decorations and prepared for the upcoming two months with my cat buddies in Roussillon. As I gathered things to take to Paul and Anne's, I was ruthless in sorting and dropped a couple bags of clothing into the Red Cross bin. I was getting ready for a really NEW year, and I didn't want to be dragging a lot of old baggage, be it tangible objects or emotions.

I'd first taken care of Paul and Anne's cats in 2007 for Christmas. Each year thereafter, I'd done a Christmas gig and then additional weeks in January and February. How fast those years had gone! I missed Sebby, but Ellie had grown friendlier, and even Frankie, as she'd gotten older, was hanging around more.

I had less than two months to prepare for my extended stay in Florida. Meg graciously said I could store things in the apartment, but I wanted to reduce the amount of stuff I had accumulated. I did not know what the upcoming summer months would bring, or how my future time in the Luberon would evolve. I was ruthless in culling clothing and other items I'd accumulated. Coats I hadn't worn in two (mild) winters went into the Red Cross drop box. Extra pots, pans, and cookware were donated to an organization in Apt helping the homeless and disadvantaged.

Gathering paperwork for renewal of the *Carte* went smoothly.

After twelve years, I'd gotten it down to a routine. I asked Brigitte to take me to the Préfecture in Avignon. Mid-week we met in Apt and she drove me to the Préfecture. I'd applied for my first *Carte de Séjour* in 2004. Over the years, I'd asked what I could do to get a card valid for longer than a year. The response had steadfastly been the same, "Do you own property in France?" "No." "Do you pay taxes in France?" "No." "Then you need to renew every year."

This year, the process was speedier than usual. I had not made an appointment, opting instead to take a number and wait. I was promptly ushered into one of the backroom cubicles. An extremely efficient woman whisked me through the process, which now required finger printing. She proceeded to ask a series of questions about my income and length of time I spent in France. She acted very surprised that I did not have a card valid for longer than a year and said she was going to put a request in for me. I explained the reasons I'd been given in the past, but she appeared to think my age and income qualified for a longer-term card. Who was I to argue?

I thanked her, and twenty minutes later I joined Brigitte in the parking lot, and we were on our way to Saignon. I just shook my head. I'd ceased trying to understand bureaucracy in France and crossed my fingers. Of course, I'd be back in the States when the new card arrived, and only trusted they'd hold it for me when I came back in the fall or winter, as they had in the past. I could never be completely certain of how anything would unfold where the French government was concerned. All I could to was hope and pray and wait and see.

I communicated regularly with Joe and Sally and learned they'd decided to go back to Michigan for the summer. They would not go as far north as Traverse City, but had opted to rent a house in Ann Arbor, where they had lived prior to moving north to Glen Arbor. I'd been fiddling around with renting a house for the summer in Florida, and their plans played into my hands. We agreed I'd rent their house while they were gone. My housing need was solved, and they wouldn't have to leave their house empty or trust it to the hands of strangers.

April 30, 2016

Clear and sunny and no wind! Went to Apt yesterday afternoon and dropped things at the donation site. Packed one suitcase with all my winter things. Helped Meg rake more leaves on the terrace. Such mixed feelings about the upcoming months and beyond. A part of me wants to stay and part of me wants to leave. I am still the little girl whose father thought she should have been born twins.

THE SUNDAY BEFORE DEPARTURE, I went to lunch at Mireille and Jean-Claude's. We had an aperitif, and nibbles, followed by Mireille's authentic Moroccan Couscous. We enjoyed dessert and coffee, then said teary good-byes. I promised to keep in touch via email.

May 17, 2016   DEPARTURE DAY!

Yesterday I walked the vineyard with Meg and Miel. Later had lunch with Meg. She's taking me to the TGV in Avignon this afternoon. Au revoir Luberon … Saignon … France!

51 Reflection - 2018

USUALLY, WHEN YOU START OUT to tell a story, you know how it ends. In this case, I did not and do not. I do know what I've learned since that winter of 2003, when I first set foot on the Domaine des Claparèdes.

When I look back on the past fifteen-plus years, I do so with no small amount of surprise. In a way I feel as if I'm reviewing someone else's life. But it's mine. I do wonder what might have been had breast cancer not come along and effectively canceled my chances of having my very own house in the Luberon, which I had desperately wanted for so many years. If I called the French couple, would the little house in Buoux, once again be available? Yet, even if it were, I know I'm no longer ready to spend extended periods of time away from family. As I've aged, so have they, and it feels more important to be geographically close.

I've rented a house in The Villages for the coming year and maybe beyond. I've found my stateside version of Megaform, a sports club, where I participate in regular exercise classes, and I'm meeting new friends there just as I met Brigitte and Nicole in France.

I survived Hurricane Irma earlier this year and added that experience to the list of things I'm learning about life in Florida. I watch the Sandhill Cranes prance around the windows of my house and listen to their strangely mournful cries.

As I contemplate spending less time in France, and after so many years of the annual onerous task getting my long-term stay *Carte de Séjour,* this last time I was finally granted a *Carte de Résident,* which does not expire until 2026. Talk about ironic!

I make visits to Michigan where I stay with Melissa, who continues to be that cross between best friend and the daughter I never had. She, and her new feline resident, Tyler Marie, are very much a part of my life.

I stay in touch with friends in France. Meg and I communicate fairly often via email and once in a while via FaceTime. Paul and Anne write and have found good house and pet sitters, so I no longer feel the pang of guilt I felt initially when I decided that this winter, for the first time since 2007, I would not be spending the Christmas holiday in the Luberon caring for the cats. I may have been reliable, but I'm not indispensable.

Michael and Susan still have their expansive, beautiful house in the country outside of Apt but at the same time are restoring a gorgeous old manse in the heart of Apt. They write often of their progress. Both Orlando and Pussycat are skipping around the great catnip field on high.

Photographer Gene maintains contact via email, and he and his wife are planning another trip to France with a stay in Saignon. I hope he sends more of his extraordinary photos.

I stay in contact with Mireille and with Nicole via email and Facebook. They both will always be my "French family," even an ocean away. The years have taught me that distance doesn't matter with true friendship. I see how some who once were closer have faded into the background, and that's really all right. I haven't set eyes on Lizzie or Andrew for many years. They opened the door for me to my life in France, but it closed behind them; they are a part of my past.

In the spring of 2017, I went back to the Domaine des Claparèdes for a six-week stay. It was at once déjà vu and an entirely new experience. The German owners have continued improvements, and the property looked superb. The lilacs were in bloom and the forsythia brilliant yellow. The little cottage I rented was not *Le Potager* I'd occupied, but rather the one they call *La Petite Maison*, the little house sitting quietly on the edge of the ever-present lavender field with Mt. Ventoux looming in the distance. There was only one resident cat named Didier, who, while not tame, did visit my patio for his daily ration of kibble.

Nicole and Shona came for walks around the grounds. Meg visited often and sometimes brought Miel to stay for the day with her Auntie Jo Anne. Mireille and Jean-Claude also stopped by, and we reminisced about the days of Lizzie and Andrew.

I no longer have the Old Gray Mare. After I left France, Jean-Claude sold the car for me. New laws mean she would no longer pass the required testing to be declared road worthy. So now, I have no car either there or here. I have my reliable golf cart as my main means of transportation in The Villages. When that doesn't suffice, Joe and/or Sally take me in their car, or I phone the reliable taxi service.

I've learned I'm essentially a person who requires solitude in large doses. I remember that first winter at the Claparèdes, when I'd gaze at the stars and feel a sense of peace and contentment. It was then I first realized, as much as I love people and enjoy being with others,

I need my alone time. There's a difference between solitude and loneliness. I am not lonely.

What these years have done is reinforce my trust in my own intuition and my firm belief, instilled in me by my mother, that I can really do almost anything I put my mind to doing. It also has taught me I cannot "go it alone." I need family and friends, the support of both, and I crave the unconditional love of pets. I take care of Will from time to time, when Joe and Sally want to be away. I follow the adventures of little Shona and Miel as well as Paul and Anne's cats, Ellie and Frankie.

I still love France and all it represents for me: a sense of permanence, a respect for history and people. I'll go back to the Domaine des Claparèdes next spring for a few weeks. Shorter stays now feel better than extended periods, but I'm not yet ready never to return.

I get weepy when I remember my dear, sweet Beemer and Snowy as well as Sebby. When I think of my friends Rod and Stephen, I'm reminded of Flavia Weeden's words: "Some people come into our lives and quickly go. Some stay for a while, leave footprints on our hearts, and we are never, ever the same." I think the same can be said for pets.

I'm no longer asking myself, "Where is home?" I've come to believe that I'm the perfect snail. I carry my home on my back.

Free and easy, that's my style
Howdy-do me, watch me smile
Fare-thee-well me after a while
'Cause I gotta roam
And any place I hang my hat is home

There's a voice in the lonesome wind
That keeps whisp'ring, "Roam!"
I'm going where a welcome mat is
No matter where that is
'Cause any place I hang my hat is home

— Johnny Mercer

ACKNOWLEDGEMENTS

Thanks to Mardi Link for her superb editing and guidance as I wrote this story. To Doug Weaver for helping fine-tune the manuscript and designer Heather Lee Shaw for seeing it to print. A *grand merci* to all my friends in France, who welcomed me and allowed me to be a part of their lives. Most are mentioned by name, others are not, but you are all appreciated. To Gene Turner, whose superb photos add so much to the story and for his friendship and talent. Finally, to my brother, Joe, and sister-in-law, Sally, who supported me during this adventure and continue to do so as I make my way along life's paths.

ABOUT THE AUTHOR

Jo Anne Wilson was born and raised in Michigan. She was a French teacher and career educator who never wrote anything other than lesson plans until she retired. Her first foray into creative writing was a book about living in Northern Michigan, called *Walks With Maggie*. Currently spending time in Southern France, Northern Michigan and Central Florida, she is working on a follow up book, *Letters from France*.

Made in the USA
Lexington, KY
13 March 2018